A FUNNY THING

HAPPENED ON THE WAY

TO THE WHITE HOUSE

EDITED *and with an* INTRODUCTION *by*

CHARLES OSGOOD

HYPERION

NEW YORK

A FUNNY THING

HAPPENED

ON THE WAY

TO THE

WHITE HOUSE

Humor, Blunders, and Other Oddities
from the Presidential Campaign Trail

Library of Congress Cataloging-in-
Publication Data is available upon request.

ISBN: 978-1-4013-2229-8

Hyperion books are available for special
promotions, premiums, or corporate
training. For details contact Michael
Rentas, Proprietary Markets, Hyperion,
77 West 66th Street, 12th floor,
New York, New York 10023,
or call 212-456-0133.

Design by Karen Minster

FIRST EDITION

10 9 8 7 6 5 4 3 2 1

Contents

Introduction

Too many of us think that running for president is serious business, and for the most part that is true. But there is another side to running for president—the funny, unpredictable, humorous side.

Without humor, politics—and those seeking the highest office in the land—would be pretty dull. Not all the humor in this book is deliberate of course; much is either accidental or off the cuff, but all of it is remarkably entertaining, from "I am Al Gore, and I used to be the next president of the United States of America," to George W. Bush's, "If you're sick and tired of the politics of cynicism and polls and principles, come and join this campaign."

In the following pages you will find quips, quotes, and comments from those running for office as well as those who observe the process and put in their two cents, such as veteran comedian/curmudgeon Mort Sahl who was so displeased by the 1960 election that pitted John F. Kennedy against Richard Nixon that he was forced to say, "I don't think that either candidate will win."

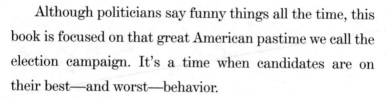

Although politicians say funny things all the time, this book is focused on that great American pastime we call the election campaign. It's a time when candidates are on their best—and worst—behavior.

Perhaps it is true we can learn more from a witty remark than a ponderous speech.

You be the judge—cast your vote.

Charles Osgood
NEW YORK

A FUNNY THING HAPPENED ON THE WAY TO THE WHITE HOUSE

THE ELECTION OF 1948

HARRY S. TRUMAN, Democrat
24.2 million (303 electoral) Alben W. Barkley

THOMAS E. DEWEY, Republican
22 million (189 electoral) Earl Warren

J. STROM THURMOND, States' Rights Dem.
1.2 million (39 electoral) Fielding L. Wright

HENRY A. WALLACE, Progressive
1.2 million (0 electoral) Glen Taylor

NORMAN THOMAS, Socialist
139,572 (0 electoral) Tucker P. Smith

This election turned out to be the greatest election upset in U.S. history. Although almost every scientific and informal poll had Dewey the winner, Truman triumphed. Even newspapers were fooled, and the photo of Truman holding the *Chicago Daily Tribune* with the headline touting *DEWEY DEFEATS TRUMAN* is an American icon. Shocked by his defeat, Dewey later said he felt like the man who woke up to find himself inside a coffin with a lily in his hand and thinking: "If I'm alive, what am I doing here? And if I'm dead, why do I have to go to the bathroom?"

This election was also famous because it brought us the first "sound bites," short quips that suited Truman's quick in-and-out style of campaigning in small towns. Because the whistle stops were short, Truman relied on pithy, clever, and succinct comments and phrases to get his points across—and have them stick. For example, Truman jabbed Republicans with this one:

"Republicans don't like people to talk about depressions. You remember the old saying: 'Don't talk about rope in the house of somebody who has to be hanged.'" And, Truman said of undeclared voters, "Whenever a man tells me he is bipartisan, I know he is going to vote against me."

When President Franklin D. Roosevelt died in office on April 12, 1945, just as World War II was ending, Vice President Harry S. Truman was thrust into a public office for which he was unprepared. He had been vice president only a year, and unlike contemporary vice presidents who have expanded that office, he was poorly informed about foreign policy. Facing him was the Soviet Union, which was growing hostile and increasing its influence in Eastern Europe.

Truman acknowledged his lack of experience to reporters when he said, "Boys, if you ever pray, pray for me now. I don't know whether you fellows ever had a load of hay fall on you, but when they told me yesterday what had happened [Roosevelt's death], I felt like the moon, the stars, and all the planets had fallen on me."

Although Truman got the Democratic nomination, the Republican candidate Thomas E. Dewey seemed like a shoo-in because of the unraveling of the Democratic Party and widespread unhappiness both with Truman's foreign and domestic policies.

Truman's strategy was to reach out to as many voters as possible, and he covered 20,000 miles, delivering about 250 speeches with his down-home style. Dewey's strategy was somewhat the opposite. Republican leaders were so sure of his victory that they had him lay low, avoid major mistakes, and offer only watered-down comments to which no one could take offense.

Truman said of his bid for president:

"My choice early in life was either to be a piano player in a whorehouse or a politician. And to tell the truth, there's hardly any difference."

During a campaign speech Truman, paraphrasing Mark Twain, noted:

"Suppose you were an idiot. And suppose you were a Republican. But I repeat myself."

An editorial in *The Courier-Journal* (Louisville, Kentucky) summed up Dewey's strategy of avoiding controversy and saying very little of substance:

"No presidential candidate [Dewey] in the future will be so inept that four of his major speeches can be boiled down to these historic four sentences: Agriculture is important. Our rivers are full of fish. You cannot have freedom without liberty. Our future lies ahead." (Dewey actually said all of these "earth-shattering" things.)

And Dewey himself summed up his strategy with this:

"When you're leading, don't talk."

From a Truman campaign speech in Dexter, Iowa:

"I heard a fellow tell a story about how he felt when he had to make speeches. He said when he has to make a speech, he felt like the fellow who was at the funeral of his wife, and the undertaker had asked him if he would ride down to the cemetery in the same car with his mother-in-law. He said, 'Well, I can do it, but it's just going to spoil the whole day for me.'"

LOCAL COLOR

"Vote for the Crook. It's important."
—*A bumper sticker for Edwin Edwards, in his successful
1991 campaign against David Duke for governor of
Louisiana. Edwards was widely considered corrupt and
later served ten years in prison. Duke was leader of the Ku
Klux Klan, and Edwards was thought by some to be the
lesser of two evils.*

"Anyone can be elected governor. I'm proof of that."
—*Joe Frank Harris (governor of Georgia, 1983–1991)*

Said Truman of his opponent:

"Herbert Hoover once ran on the slogan 'Two cars in
every garage!'

"Apparently the Republican candidate this year is running on the slogan 'Two families in every garage.'"

Truman said this about his very extensive campaign schedule:

"Cut your speech to twenty-five minutes, shake hands
with as many people as you can for a little while. Afterward,
even if you have time left, leave. If you have no place to go,
you can always pull off the road and take a nap."

Of Dewey's less extensive touring schedule, Truman noted:

"You have to get around and listen to what people are

saying. Dewey learned that in '48. He didn't listen, he just talked and didn't say much, either."

One of the most famous Trumanisms was "Give 'em Hell, Harry." To this he explained:

"I never did give anybody hell. I just told the truth, and they thought it was hell."

Truman liked to tell of campaigning on an Indian reservation. After each promise of what he'd do for Indians if elected, the crowd shouted, "Oompah! Oompah!" The louder this chorus grew, the more inspired Truman's speech became. As he left, the president had to cross a corral that had been filled with horses. "Careful," his Indian escort told him. "Don't step in the oompah."

Truman tried to deflate the polls that showed Dewey ahead. In Cleveland, Ohio, Truman said:

"These polls that the Republican candidate is putting out are like sleeping pills designed to lull the voters into sleeping on election day. You might call them sleeping polls."

Truman employed the same strategy used by Roosevelt of not mentioning your opponent by name:

"In most of my campaigns, I find it best not to mention my opponent by name because, by doing so, it just gives him the chance to get into the headlines."

Truman noted sarcastically:

"When a leader is in the Democratic Party, he's a boss; when he's in the Republican Party, he's a leader."

Again, Truman took aim at polls that put Dewey in the lead:
"It isn't important who is ahead at one time or another in either an election or a horse race. It's the horse that comes in first at the finish that counts."

"I was supremely confident of your defeat," Truman's friend George Allen said after the election. "So was everybody else," said Truman. "But you're the first one who's admitted it."

LOCAL COLOR

"You think you are so smart. I'll tell you how smart I am. I went all the way through USL [the University of Southwestern Louisiana] and I have never read a book all the way through."
—*Paul Hardy (1991 Louisiana gubernatorial candidate)*

"I think he's a very moral man. I think he's very Christian."
—*Philip Giordano, 2000 senatorial candidate from Connecticut, on his Jewish opponent, Joe Lieberman*

Senator Robert Taft once said of Dewey:
"You really have to get to know Dewey to dislike him."

Soon after his election, Truman decided not to run again.

"If you don't like the heat, get out of the kitchen," he told a friend, using one of his favorite phrases. "Well, that's what I'm doing."

On his decision not to run for a second term, Truman noted:

"If I had known how much packing I'd have to do, I'd have run again."

Many years after the election, Speaker of the House Tip O'Neill spoke about the great upset of 1948:

"I took my own informal politician's poll. I talked to fifty-six people. All fifty-six said that they didn't think that Truman could win, but all fifty-six said they were voting for Truman."

After the election comedian Groucho Marx declared:

"The only way a Republican will get into the White House is to marry Margaret Truman."

After *The Washington Post* and many other newspapers declared that Dewey would be elected, the *Post* placed a sign outside their building that read MR. PRESIDENT, WE ARE READY TO EAT CROW WHENEVER YOU ARE READY TO SERVE IT.

Humorist James Thurber said this in a piece he called "The Dewey Dewey Fog":

"Now, it seems to me that Dewey is going to be thrown for a heavy loss. Maybe even back of the 44-yard line, if he doesn't change his tactics. For if Dewey is trying to out-Truman Truman, and Truman is trying to out-Wallace Wallace, a lot of voters will jump to the conclusion that Dewey Dewey—I mean Dewey—is trying to out-Wallace Wallace. As a matter of fact, he probably intends only to out-Truman the Truman who is trying to out-Roosevelt Roosevelt, and not the Truman who is trying to out-Wallace Wallace, but this may not be clear to the Frightened Fringe, that formidable body of voters who are afraid they may inadvertently cast their ballots for a man who wants to out-Stalin Stalin."

Another humorist, H. L. Mencken, said of Truman's campaign:

"If there had been any formidable body of cannibals in the country, Harry Truman would have promised to provide them with free missionaries fattened at the taxpayers' expense."

Dewey finally realized, too late however, that he did not make enough appearances in front of voters. After the election, he and his family took a vacation in Arizona, where he rested after the campaign ordeal. One day he went behind his hotel, took off his coat, rolled up his sleeves, squatted, and began pitching pennies with his two sons. When his wife warned him that photographers might catch him in an undignified pose, he responded: "Maybe, if I had done this during the campaign, I might have won."

Truman had this to say about women in politics, as he said much later in *McCall's* magazine, September 1962:

"Women have been in everything else—why not in politics? There's no reason why a woman shouldn't be in the White House as president, if she wants to be. But she'll be sorry when she gets there."

Dewey maintained his adamant stance on not running for president. In a letter to his campaign manager while in office, Dewey wrote:

"My decision on this matter is as certain and final as death and the staggering New Deal taxes."

THE ELECTION OF 1952

DWIGHT D. EISENHOWER, Republican
33.9 million (442 electoral) Richard M. Nixon

ADLAI E. STEVENSON, Democrat
27.3 million (89 electoral) John J. Sparkman

With the entrance of Adlai E. Stevenson into the presidential campaign, the voters enjoyed the amusing wordplay of one of the country's most erudite, self-effacing, and downright funny political candidates. In fact, after he lost the election, Stevenson began a speech with: "A funny thing happened to me on the way to the White House . . ."! Stevenson also appreciated the absurdity of the election process when he noted: "In America, any boy may become president . . . and I suppose that's just the risk he takes."

Some observers, however, suggested that he was too clever, too much of an egghead, and that his humor only played to a more educated crowd. That's not entirely true, but this complaint resonated with voters who chose a war hero instead.

The Republicans were looking to end the Democratic domination of the presidency that began with FDR's first term in 1932. Who would be a more powerful contender than General Dwight Eisenhower, Supreme Commander of NATO, the man responsible for the D-Day invasion and beating the Nazi terror? In 1951, after turning down previous offers to run for president, he finally agreed to throw his helmet in the ring. Even then, he held back placing his name on primary ballots until he saw himself winning on write-in ballots.

Truman had made it quite clear that he would not run for reelection, and several possible candidates popped up, including W. Averill Harriman, Truman's commerce secretary, Senator Estes Kefauver, and vice president Alben Barkley. Although he had originally declined to run, Illinois governor Adlai Stevenson was eventually drafted as the Democratic nominee based on his excellent keynote speech at the convention.

This election was the first one in which television became a factor both in broadcasting speeches and in advertising candidates. It also played a role in Richard Nixon defending himself against allegations that he had a secret slush fund. He used the tube to deliver what was called his "Checkers Speech" because he used the dog, given as a gift to his daughter, to deflect attention away from the real issue—his honesty (more on the speech later).

Eisenhower ingratiated himself with voters when, less than a month before the election, he vowed to go to Korea and end the two-year-old stalemate. He used the opportunity to criticize Truman for removing American troops from Korea in 1949, which emboldened the North Koreans to attack in June 1950. He also chided Truman for being soft on Communism in his dealings with the Soviet Union.

Adlai Stevenson, meanwhile, proved to be one of the most eloquent candidates ever. He was witty and quick on his feet, and offered thoughtful analysis of the issues. Unfortunately, that's not what the voters wanted.

Not only was the election the first to use television, but it was the first election in which candidates' medical records were made public. This became a factor in later elections after Eisenhower suffered a heart attack in 1955, a year before standing for reelection in 1956.

. . . .

Eisenhower often told the story of the man who urged him to run for Senate. He said to the man in a self-deprecating manner:

"My gosh, no! The truth alone would beat me—not to mention what the opposition would say about me."

Eisenhower likened running a campaign to the D-Day invasion:

"I'm beginning to realize that organizing a presidential campaign is about as intricate as planning a large-scale invasion across an ocean barrier."

Eisenhower was not above the one-line zinger, this time comparing politics to war:

"The Democratic Party is not one, but two political parties with the same name. They unite only once every two years—to wage political campaigns."

For Nixon to become a viable vice-presidential candidate, he had to convince the American public that he was not a crook, that he had not taken any money for political favors. In the famous "Checkers Speech," Nixon used the camera to his advantage and explained about the incident involving $18,000 given to him by supporters. He went into sympathetic detail about his family life, how much a senator made

($15,000 annually), and how he and his wife, Pat, saved for a house. He ended with the following heart-tugging section for which the speech is remembered:

"One other thing I probably should tell you, because if I don't, they'll probably be saying this about me, too. We did get something, a gift, after the election. A man down in Texas heard Pat on the radio mention the fact that our two youngsters would like to have a dog. And believe it or not, the day before we left on this campaign trip, we got a message from Penn Station in Baltimore, saying they had a package for us. We went down to get it. You know what it was? It was a little cocker spaniel dog in a crate that he'd sent all the way from Texas—black and white, spotted. And our little girl Tricia, the six-year-old, named it Checkers. And you know, the kids, like all kids, love the dog, and I just want to say this, right now, that regardless of what they say about it, we're gonna keep it."

LOCAL COLOR

"It's on at the same time as *Entertainment Tonight*."
—*Republican Jeb Bush, governor of Florida, explaining why he wasn't planning to watch the debate between his two Democratic opponents for governor of Florida in 2002*

"I have a reputation for being strait-laced, but actually I come from a very tough state—Utah. Do you think it's easy raising money from people who are all sober?"
—*Utah senator Orrin Hatch*

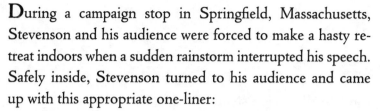

During a campaign stop in Springfield, Massachusetts, Stevenson and his audience were forced to make a hasty retreat indoors when a sudden rainstorm interrupted his speech. Safely inside, Stevenson turned to his audience and came up with this appropriate one-liner:

"I really wanted to save you from drowning next January."

In Pontiac, Michigan, Stevenson gave up trying to give a speech in a downpour that drenched about a thousand people.

"I'm not going to talk to you about labor policies," began Stevenson. "I'm not going to talk to you about foreign policies. In fact, I'm not going to talk to you about a thing, because of this damned rain. Good-bye!"

The crowd laughed and dispersed.

Stevenson was defending himself continually against those who said he spoke only to the most educated voters. Here, he took the criticism head-on:

"If I talk over the people's head, Ike must be talking under their feet."

Stevenson made note of the relatively new use of scientific polls in elections:

"Now, as usual, my friends, the preelection thunder comes from the Republicans. They have most of the nation's newspapers and magazines. They have the slickest slogans and the shiniest posters. They win most of the preelection polls, and sometimes they win them in a 'Gallup.' It is not a very good pun, but it is the best I could do."

In his own way, Stevenson chided the Republican Party for the deal that reportedly occurred between Senator Taft and Eisenhower that allowed Ike to be nominated for president. The two agreed that Taft, a powerful party leader, would stay out of foreign affairs and Eisenhower would follow a conservative domestic policy.

"General Eisenhower employs the three-monkeys standard of campaign morality: See no evil—if it's Republican; hear no evil—unless it is Democratic; and speak no evil—unless Senator Taft says it's all right."

Despite the agreement between Taft and Eisenhower, there was disharmony between the moderate East Coast establishment represented by Eisenhower and the conservative GOP wing led by Taft. After a well-publicized peace conference with Taft, Eisenhower said that party harmony was the first objective of the Republicans, to which the Democratic opponent Stevenson noted:

"I shall not argue that it is necessarily fatal to change horses in midstream. But I doubt if it is wise to jump on the struggling two-headed elephant trying to swim in both directions at the same time."

As governor of Illinois, Stevenson welcomed the 1952 Democratic National Convention with these words:

"I have a notion the voters are going to respond in November to those Republican promises the way a certain young lady responded to the proposal of a young farmer friend of hers. He said, 'Marry me and I'll paint the house and the barn inside and out. I'll put in electricity, I'll buy

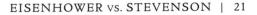

a brand-new stove and refrigerator. Will you marry me?' And she said, 'Honey, let's leave it this way, you do all those things and then ask me again.'"

On December 13, 1952, a month after he was defeated by Dwight D. Eisenhower in his first race for president, Adlai Stevenson addressed the annual gathering of Washington reporters at the Gridiron Club:

"A funny thing happened to me on the way to the White House . . . !

"The fact was, of course, that the general was so far ahead, we never even saw him. I was happy to hear I had even placed second. But no one will say, I trust, that I snatched defeat from the jaws of victory. . . . Now I content myself that it is all for the best. After all, didn't Socrates say that the duty of a man of real principle is to stay out of politics? So you see I'm delighted that the sovereign people have put an even higher value on my principles than I did. . . . I have great faith in the people. As to their wisdom, well, Coca-Cola still outsells champagne. They make mistakes. They do sometimes. But given time they correct their mistakes—at two- or four-year intervals.

"I have faith in the people—and in their chosen leaders: men of high purpose, goodwill, and humble hearts, men quite prepared to stand aside when the time comes and allow even more humble men to take over."

Stevenson often attacked the Republicans for what he considered their disinterest in the common voter and focus on rich people.

"Whenever the Republicans talk of cutting taxes first and discussing the national security second, they remind me of a very tired, rich man who said to his chauffeur: 'Drive off that cliff, James, I want to commit suicide.' "

LOCAL COLOR

"You need a little more decaf."
—*Arnold Schwarzenegger to the high-energy Arianna Huffington during a gubernatorial debate*

"Here's the kitchen. Here's the hallway. We've got plenty of closet space. Look, no skeletons."
—*Russ Feingold, Senate candidate from Wisconsin during a campaign ad showing his home*

Replying to Republican criticism that he used wit in his speeches that was too "highbrow," Stevenson said:

"In a recent speech in Indianapolis, Senator Taft made an attempt at his own brand of campaign humor. He said, laughingly, that he and Senator Jenner and Senator Capehart, the author of the Capehart Amendment, should get together after this speech and decide on campaign policy. If they want to make an issue of campaign humor, let's put that joke at the head of the list. If it is a crime to trust the people's common sense and native intelligence, I gladly plead guilty,

I've just been trying to give the customers the right change. That seems to be novel and effete."

Upon noting that the platform from which the Republican candidate was addressing a Richmond audience had collapsed, Mr. Stevenson commented:

"I'm glad the general wasn't hurt. But I wasn't surprised that it happened. I've been telling him for two months that nobody could stand on that platform."

Stevenson said of Eisenhower, who was asked many times to dedicate buildings, bridges, and other public structures:

"The general has dedicated himself so many times, he must feel like the cornerstone of a public building."

In Fort Dodge, Iowa, Stevenson came up with this:

"The Republicans have a 'me too' candidate running, a 'yes but' platform, advised by a 'has been' staff."

In Bakersfield, California, Stevenson noted:

"I have been tempted to make a proposal to our Republican friends: that if they stop telling lies about us, we would stop telling the truth about them." (This quip gets repeated often by various candidates in future elections.)

Again, Stevenson tried to show that Eisenhower was not his own man:

"Senator Taft is the greatest living authority on what General Eisenhower thinks."

At the University of Wisconsin, Stevenson said:

"It makes me shudder to think that I graduated from college thirty years ago and how doddering and venerable the thirtieth reunion class looked to me then. If I look to you the way they looked to me, I wouldn't vote for me! Having uttered that sentence, I quickly comfort myself by reminding you that you haven't any younger alternatives."

In his self-deprecating way, Stevenson said:

"I have been in politics barely four years. There are some politicians who don't think I'm in yet, and others who expect me to be out of it very soon."

To illustrate how he felt losing the presidency while his fellow Democrats swept control of Congress, Stevenson told the story of the Lone Ranger riding the Western plains with his ever-faithful Indian sidekick, Tonto. The story has been told many times since then:

"Suddenly, they were encircled by hostile Indians—a thousand Sioux to the front, three thousand Iroquois to the rear, and two thousand Apaches on either side. The Lone Ranger turned to Tonto and said, 'It looks bad for us, old pal.' To which Tonto replied, 'What do you mean, "us," white man?' "

Stevenson attacked Nixon many times:

"Nixon is the kind of politician who would cut down a redwood tree, then mount the stump for a speech on conservation."

Speaking of the Republican party, Mr. Stevenson quipped:

"The elephant has a thick skin, a head full of ivory, and as everyone who has seen a circus parade knows, proceeds best by grasping the tail of his predecessor."

LOCAL COLOR

"Have you ever seen a candidate talking to a rich person on television?"
—*Art Buchwald, political satirist*

"I think it proves that North Carolina doesn't want a senator who knows how to cuss."
—*Bo Thomas, after losing his bid for the Senate from North Carolina in 1976*

When he lost the election, Stevenson said of the vote:

"As Abraham Lincoln said, I feel 'like a little boy who had stubbed his toe in the dark . . . he was too old to cry, but it hurt too much to laugh.'"

Stevenson had trouble understanding why voters seemed to like candidates who portrayed themselves as folksy instead of smart:

"The hardest thing about any political campaign is how to win without proving that you are unworthy of winning."

Informed by academics that he enjoyed "the support of all thinking Americans," Stevenson joked, "That's not enough. I'm going to need a majority."

The absurdity of being president was not lost on Stevenson:

"They pick a president, and then for four years they pick *on* him."

At a meeting of New York's Liberal Party Stevenson said:

"In my very brief political career I've sometimes wondered if I had any friends left. And then they suddenly nominated me for president, and I wondered if I hadn't too many."

Stevenson found it absurd that people expected perfection in their presidential candidate:

"If the candidate purported to know the right answer to everything, he would be either a knave or a fool. . . . If he should arrive at election time with almost everybody satisfied, then you should, by all means, vote against him as the most dangerous charlatan of them all."

Stevenson said that campaigning was extremely rigorous:

"You must write [speeches] at every chance, think if possible, and ride through city after city on the back of an open car, smiling until your mouth is dehydrated by the wind, waving until the blood runs out of your arms . . . bounce gaily, confidently, masterfully into great howling halls . . . You must [read a speech] so defaced with chicken tracks that you couldn't follow it, even if the spotlights weren't blinding and even if the photographers didn't shoot you in the eye every time you looked at them."

Stevenson made fun of Republicans with this clever comment:

"I like a lot of Republicans. . . . Indeed, there are some Republicans I would trust with anything—anything, that is, except public office."

In the era of McCarthyism, Stevenson answered attacks that he favored "creeping Socialism." His response:

"I am no more in favor of Socialism than anybody else, and I particularly dislike things that creep. But if I don't like what they call creeping Socialism, there is something else I dislike just as much, and that is galloping reaction."

An aide once told Stevenson that it cost $60,000 to put one of his speeches on TV.

The candidate responded:

"I wish you hadn't told me. Now every time I start to put a word on paper, I'll wonder whether it's an expensive, ten-dollar word or a little, unimportant word like 'is' or 'and' that costs only a dollar seventy-five."

Of the McCarthy–Jenner endorsement of Eisenhower, Stevenson said:

"This is the first time I've heard a party campaigning on the slogan, 'Throw the Rascals In.'"

Stevenson criticized what he considered inconsistencies in the Republican platform:

"I have not changed my views to suit my itinerary. I have not talked titles in Texas, corruption in California, and love in Louisiana. I have not been a 'sunflower' candidate, turning my face as needs be to catch the fullest rays of the voters' favor."

The humor did not end when the election was over. To reporters after his defeat he said:

"Come in and have some fried postmortems on toast."

Once again, commenting on his defeat in 1952, Adlai Stevenson made these comments about his presidential campaign:

"Thousands even wrote gracious, flattering letters after the election, explaining why they did not vote for me. They seemed to feel they owed me an explanation. I was touched and flattered, but I confess the thought occurred to me now and then that a little 'X' in the right place on the ballot would have been so much easier than a long, thoughtful letter."

Stevenson said of politicians:

"A politician is a person who approaches every subject with an open mouth."

Ike's aide, Sherman Adams, and his wife voted in New York on election day and then visited the Bronx Zoo. When they returned to the Commodore Hotel that evening to await the returns with Eisenhower, they told how they had just come from the zoo. "Quite a change from a political campaign," someone in the room said. "No, not much," said Mrs. Adams.

LOCAL COLOR

"Vote early and vote often."
—*James Michael Curley, mayor of Boston from 1914 to 1934
(this quote in similar forms has been attributed to many
other politicians)*

"As we all know, the truth is a frequent casualty in the
heat of an election campaign."
—*Speaker Tip O'Neill, 55th Speaker of the House*

From a column in the *New York Post*, Robert Bendiner
wrote of the primaries:

"What Harold Stassen and Adlai Stevenson have in
common is that people don't take them seriously—Stassen
when he says he's running and Stevenson when he says he
isn't.

"They call these contests 'preferential' primaries because
you can interpret them any way you prefer. If you get the
most votes in a primary, you win; if you aren't soundly
trounced, you've scored a moral victory; and if you're thor-
oughly whipped, you weren't really running in the first place.

"Pins are being devised for Taft people here reading: 'I
don't like Ike yet but I'm working on it.'

"The most recent poll of Harry Truman shows that 36
percent of him wants to run, 34 percent does not, 18 percent
doesn't know, and 12 percent knows but won't tell."

The 1952 election saw for the first time the use of television ads often created by high profile advertising agencies such as BBD&O. Here writer and critic Marya Mannes, known for her biting but perceptive observations of American life, penned this poem:

SALES CAMPAIGN

Hail to B.B.D. & O.
It told the nation how to go;
It managed by advertisement
To sell us a new President.
Eisenhower hits the spot,
One full general, that's a lot.
Feeling sluggish, feeling sick?
Take a dose of Ike and Dick.
Philip Morris, Lucky Strike,
Alka-Seltzer, I like Ike.

THE ELECTION OF 1956

DWIGHT D. EISENHOWER, Republican
35.6 million (457 electoral) Richard M. Nixon

ADLAI STEVENSON, Democrat
27.3 million (73 electoral) Estes Kefauver

To say that Stevenson was running into a brick wall would be an understatement, but he kept his sense of humor. While campaigning, Stevenson asked some children in his audience, "How many children would like to be a candidate for president of the United States?" They raised their hands. Then Stevenson continued, "And how many candidates for president of the United States would like to be children again?" And he raised his hand.

Eisenhower was a very popular president because his first term showed some positive results. Negotiations ended the Korean War, Joseph McCarthy's war against American Communism—real or imagined—was finally over, and the Supreme Court in 1954 ruled in *Brown* v. *Board of Education of Topeka* that segregated public schools were unconstitutional. Not all people were pleased with Eisenhower's performance, of course, as evidenced by the Republicans losing control of Congress in 1954.

Personally, however, most people did like Ike, especially his anti-Communist stance in foreign policy against the growing "Red Menace" and the fact that the country was economically prosperous.

There was speculation that Eisenhower would not run for a second term because he had suffered a heart attack while in office, but when he announced he would run for re-election, the voters felt comfortable that he was healthy enough to serve.

Stevenson campaigned vigorously against frontrunner Eisenhower with both sides using television ads aimed not only at male voters but women as well. Housewives had played a large role in the 1952 election of Eisenhower, and both sides were courting that demographic.

Eisenhower ran largely on his record and portrayed the Democrats as still stuck in the 1930s, talking about the Great Depression and bad economic times. Stevenson changed his style and targeted his message at the "non-egghead" electorate, trying to counter claims that he appealed to only elite and highly educated voters. Stevenson attacked the nation's military bent, saying that the Selective Service was ineffective and unfair. He also suggested a moratorium on the testing of atomic weapons. For a country that was flexing its military muscles in the international arena in such places as Indochina, Iran, and Central America, Stevenson's "less war" message did not resonate with voters.

By the end of the campaign, the world was rocked by the Hungarian Revolution, which saw the USSR storm into Hungary to quell an uprising for freedom, and the crisis over the Suez Canal, which had Egypt locked in a fight with France, Great Britain, and Israel—all U.S. allies. The American public was comforted at having a military man in charge of the country during these unsettled times, and Eisenhower exuded strong leadership and resolve.

He won the election handily (one electoral vote from Alabama went to Walter B. Jones, a States' Rights judge from that state), and Vice President Nixon rode the popularity of President Eisenhower, although he was himself popular among the more conservative wing of the Republican Party.

. . . .

Stevenson played up the nagging feeling among voters that Richard Nixon was a dishonest person despite his weathering the Checkers incident:

"I don't wish to deprecate the vice president's [Nixon's] new personality," said Stevenson. "But I do wish that we might hear some word from him repudiating the irresponsible, vindictive, and malicious words so often spoken by the imposter who has been using his name all these years."

Eisenhower was popular, but he thought his speechwriters made him sound "too good," and sometimes asked them to tone it down. On one occasion he told them:

"Those last couple of paragraphs are fine and ringing, but I can't get away from the feeling that they make me sound like Saint Peter."

One issue that hurt Eisenhower was low farm prices. Stevenson riffed on it:

"I'm beginning to think the reason President Eisenhower decided to run again is that he just couldn't afford to retire to his farm in Gettysburg as long as Ezra Benson is Secretary of Agriculture."

LOCAL COLOR

At a black-tie dinner in Washington in 1987, Senator Jay Rockefeller spoke to a crowd that had paid $500 a plate for a fund-raiser after his successful bid for the Senate. Rockefeller lamented about spending his own money on the campaign. "Some of you might feel cheated, paying five hundred bucks for a lousy chicken dinner, but just think about me. I spent ten million dollars to get here."

Early in the campaign, a reporter asked Stevenson if he considered himself a "middle-of-the-road Democrat."

He replied:

"I am not one of those who believes that you can characterize a philosophy on public issues by slogans. I have never been sure what progressive conservatism means, or was it conservative progressivism? I have forgotten. And I am not sure what dynamic moderation or moderate dynamism means. I am not even sure what it means when one says he is a conservative in fiscal affairs and a liberal in human affairs. I assume what it means is that you will strongly recommend the building of a great many schools to accommodate the needs of our children, but not provide the money."

Stevenson disliked having to "dress down" to attract voters—literally.

During the California primary campaign Stevenson put

on a denim jacket, cowboy boots, a string necktie, and a ten-gallon hat. He rode horseback in a parade at Los Banos before delivering an address.

Afterward he told aides to get him "out of this ridiculous costume" and moaned: "God, what a man won't do to get in public office!"

The following bumper sticker was seen on cars during the election, criticizing Eisenhower for spending too much time on the golf course:

BEN HOGAN FOR PRESIDENT.

IF WE'RE GOING TO HAVE A GOLFER FOR PRESIDENT,
LET'S HAVE A GOOD ONE.

Again, Stevenson attacked Nixon's veracity in the most clever way:

"Mr. Nixon's defenders insist that although there are certain things in his record which aren't very pretty, he has, nevertheless, shown the capacity for growth and if elected will develop the character for the job. I think it unlikely, however, that the American people will want to send Mr. Nixon to the White House just on the chance that it might do him a world of good."

Eisenhower often took issue with his speechwriters:

"Gosh, someone around here is always feeding me all these 'folksy' phrases. Hell, I'm folksy enough as it is, without their trying to make matters worse."

Nixon chimed in on the race in this way:

"To substitute Mr. Stevenson for President Eisenhower would be just like putting in an eager, untried, jittery second-string quarterback into the big game of the season with the risk that he might throw a well-intentioned pass into the flat and have it intercepted for a touchdown. And this is no time to gamble with a second-stringer and leave an All-American sitting on the bench."

On the Democratic candidate, Nixon said:

"He is a pathetic Hamlet strolling across the political stage. To be or not to be—that is the question for him. And I assure you he is not going to be president of the United States."

LOCAL COLOR

"I'm sitting on the fence with both ears firmly on the ground."
—Dan Marriott, deciding whether to run for governor of Utah

"I am running for governor not because I am George and Barbara Bush's son. I am running because I am George P. and Noelle and Jeb's father."
—Jeb Bush, campaigning for governor of Florida

Stevenson said of running for office:

"The best reason I can think of for not running for

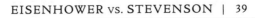

president of the United States is that you have to shave twice a day."

Comedian Mort Sahl during his act in a San Francisco nightclub:

"Eisenhower stands for 'gradualism.' Stevenson stands for 'moderation.' Between these two extremes, we the people must choose!"

THE ELECTION OF 1960

JOHN F. KENNEDY, Democrat

34.2 million (303 electoral) Lyndon B. Johnson

RICHARD M. NIXON, Republican

34.1 million (219 electoral) Henry Cabot Lodge Jr.

Some say this election was lost because of face stubble. Some of the most remembered moments of this campaign were the televised debates—the first in U.S. history—between presidential candidates. Nixon refused to wear makeup and he looked haggard. His five-o'-clock shadow made him look sinister to some. Kennedy, on the other hand, looked relaxed, strong, and charismatic.

Eisenhower was the first president to be barred by the Twenty-second Amendment from seeking a third term in office. It was just as well, because the public was starting to "Not Like Ike." His popularity was waning amidst a scandal involving his chief of staff, Sherman Adams. In addition, the country went into a recession in 1957, the same year that the Soviet Union launched *Sputnik*, the first artificial satellite, immediately putting the United States way behind in the space race.

Vice President Richard Nixon was the obvious choice for the Republican Party and had virtually no opposition. He selected former ambassador and senator Henry Cabot Lodge Jr. as his running mate.

Nixon faced John F. Kennedy, a PT boat skipper during World War II, who had beaten Lodge in the first of two successful Senate campaigns. Kennedy was the son of Joseph P.

Kennedy, who had made a fortune in many business ventures including selling liquor (both illegally during Prohibition and legally afterward), real estate, the stock market, and refinancing Hollywood studios. His son had access to his father's vast fortune to finance his campaign. John's brother, Robert, put together an efficient political organization to elect his brother. Senate Majority Leader Lyndon B. Johnson was the choice for vice president.

Kennedy's message to the voters was of a new, vibrant generation of leadership, and his young demeanor and striking wife, Jacqueline, underscored the message. Kennedy also brought a wit that was unprecedented, especially when he joked about his rich upbringing and his religion. If elected, Kennedy would be the first Roman Catholic to be president. He astutely took the issues head-on using humor. "I have just received the following telegram from my generous daddy," Kennedy said. "It says, 'Dear Jack: Don't buy a single vote more than is necessary. I'll be damned if I'm going to pay for a landslide.'" And he once commented to reporters the concern from Catholics who felt he was downplaying his beliefs. He joked, "Now I understand why Henry the Eighth set up his own church."

Kennedy accused the Republicans of being soft on Communism, citing the strong influence of the Soviet Union in Europe, Africa, and Asia, saying that there was a "missile gap" between the Soviets and the United States and that the Soviets were far ahead in the arms race. This later turned out not to be the case.

Nixon's strategy was to play up his anti-Communist background, harking back to his prosecution of Alger Hiss, an alleged Soviet spy. Nixon's unrelenting work to bring down Hiss—he was convicted in 1950 on perjury in connection with this charge—pushed Nixon's political career from the House of Representatives to Senate to vice president and finally as a presidential candidate.

Kennedy won by a slim margin (Senator Harry Byrd received fifteen electoral votes).

Because Kennedy understood the growing importance of television—and came across better than Nixon—he learned to offer clever and "on-message" sound bites that would be played on the evening news. Nixon . . . not so much.

• • • • • • • • • •

Said Kennedy of his opponent:

"When I first began this campaign, I just wanted to beat Nixon. Now I want to save the country from him."

LOCAL COLOR

Ted Kennedy tells this story: "When I ran for the U.S. Senate in 1962, I worked day and night campaigning. I won by 285,000 votes. In 1964, when I was again running for the Senate, I was flat on my back in the hospital and couldn't do any campaigning. So my wife, Joan, campaigned for me. That election I won by over a million votes, the largest margin ever in Massachusetts. I still think some people believe they elected my wife to the Senate in 1964."

Just before the Democratic Convention, a foreign diplomat asked Johnson:

"Sir, what are your real presidential ambitions?"

Johnson said:

"My highest ambition of all is to help elect some other man president, in the hope that maybe he would make me his appointments secretary."

During his political campaigns for the Senate in Massachusetts, Kennedy liked to tell the story of the little old Irish lady whose husband passed away. She came to the ward leader with the complaint that the officials wouldn't accept the answer she gave to a question they asked her about her late husband, which was "What did he die of?" When the ward leader asked her what her answer was, the little old Irish lady answered, "Sure, and he died of a Tuesday. I remember it well."

John F. Kennedy told a story about himself and two other aspirants, senators Lyndon Johnson and Stuart Symington, at the Gridiron Club Dinner:

"I dreamed about 1960 myself the other night, and I told Stuart Symington and Lyndon Johnson about it in the cloakroom yesterday. I told them how the Lord came into my bedroom, anointed my head and said, 'John Kennedy, I hereby appoint you President of the United States.' Stuart Symington said, 'That's strange, Jack, because I, too, had a similar dream last night in which the Lord anointed me and declared me, Stuart Symington, President of the United States and Outer Space.' Lyndon Johnson said, 'That's very interesting, gentlemen, because I, too, had a similar dream last night and I don't remember anointing either of you.' "

The primaries were hectic, and Kennedy used to tell his friends about his children missing him. True or not, this story made for great coverage.

"Caroline's first words were plane, good-bye, and New Hampshire, and she recently learned to say Wisconsin and West Virginia. Any day now she is expected to come out with Maryland and Oregon."

Prior to the Democratic convention, former president Truman said at a press conference that Kennedy was not his first choice for president. Kennedy was asked by the press to comment on Truman's remarks.

"The last conversation to which he referred in Independence was less precise than that. He said we must all join together to secure the best man. I did not feel that on that occasion he was asking me to step aside."

In Los Angeles, a reporter facetiously asked Kennedy: "Do you think a Protestant can be elected president in 1960?"

He replied: "If he's prepared to answer how he stands on the issue of the separation of church and state, I see no reason why we should discriminate against him."

California governor Pat Brown was talked about as a potential presidential contender in 1960, but he denied the rumors. He said: "I am not a candidate for president in 1960."

And added: "If this doesn't put me in the thick of the race, I don't know what will."

At a press conference in Des Moines during the campaign, Kennedy was asked: "What sort of qualifications would you look for in the man you would select for the next secretary of agriculture?" He answered:

"First, I think he should have been at some part of his life a farmer. Secondly, I think he should live in the Midwest United States. Thirdly, he should believe that his responsibility is to preserve the family farm and not liquidate it. Fourth, and finally, it would be helpful if he were a Democrat."

Kennedy also applied humor to comments about his Boston accent:

"Someone was kind enough, though I don't know whether he meant it kindly, to say the other night that in my campaign in California I sounded like a Truman with a Harvard accent."

Kennedy sponsored many $100-a-plate fund-raising dinners (a lot of money at the time) and he helped relieve some of the financial pain by offering this joke in Salt Lake City:

"I am deeply touched—not as deeply touched as you have been by coming to this dinner, but nevertheless, it is a sentimental occasion."

One campaign issue was that of giving ambassadorships based on political favors and not on experience or talent. (Remember that his father was ambassador to Great Britain.)

He said: "On this matter of experience, I had announced earlier this year that if successful, I would not consider campaign contributions as a substitute for experience in appointing ambassadors. Ever since I made that statement, I have not received one single cent from my father."

Like many candidates, Kennedy sought closeness with voters by commiserating with their sports teams' failures. In Harrisburg, Pennsylvania, he said:

"I'm glad to be here, because I feel a sense of kinship with the Pittsburgh Pirates. Like my candidacy, they were not given much chance in the spring."

LOCAL COLOR

"I have more skeletons in my closet than the Smithsonian."
—*Ben Jones, who played Cooter Davenport in the TV series*
The Dukes of Hazzard, *during his congressional bid from Georgia*

"It's either one of the best things I've ever done or one of the dumbest."
—*Janet Reno, former U.S. attorney general, on running for governor of Florida in 2002*

During most of the 1960 campaign, a Republican "truth squad" followed Kennedy around the country, making speeches in places where the Democratic candidate had spoken, in an effort to refute his claims. Kennedy made reference in San Diego to the practice when he said:

"Now we have five days before this campaign is over. I cannot predict what is going to happen. The 'truth squad' has been ditched. They told the truth once, and they don't let them travel around anymore."

During the last few days of the campaign, the rhetoric from Nixon was growing harsh. Kennedy responded in this way:

"Mr. Nixon in the last seven days has called me an economic ignoramus, a Pied Piper, and all the rest. I've just confined myself to calling him a Republican, but he says that is getting low."

In New York City, Kennedy pulled no punches with this one:

"I understand that Tom Dewey has just joined Dick Nixon out on the Coast to give him some last-minute strategy on how to win an election."

During the Alfred Smith Memorial Dinner in New York City, with only a few weeks until the election, Kennedy took a swipe at Nixon's integrity and honesty in a humorous way. He said:

"Mr. Nixon, like the rest of us, has had his troubles in this campaign. At one point even *The Wall Street Journal* was criticizing his tactics. That is like the *L'Osservatore Romano* [the Vatican newspaper] criticizing the Pope."

Kennedy attacked his opponent's comment about the United States producing better consumer goods than the Soviets.

"I wonder when he [Mr. Nixon] put his finger under Mr. Khrushchev's nose whether he was saying, 'I know you are ahead of us in rockets, Mr. Khrushchev, but we are ahead of you in color television.' I would just as soon look at black-and-white television and be ahead of them in rockets."

Kennedy was the first presidential candidate to campaign in Alaska, which had recently become a state. This is from a press conference there:

QUESTION: Senator, you were promised a military intelligence briefing from the president. Have you received that?

KENNEDY: Yes. I talked on Thursday morning to General Wheeler from the Defense Department.

QUESTION: What was his first name?

KENNEDY: He didn't brief me on that.

Kennedy said this of Al Smith, a Catholic and Democrat who ran unsuccessfully against Herbert Hoover in 1928:

"The vice president has claimed Al Smith for his work in his later years and I claimed him for his work in the 1928 campaign. Neither one of us indicated what Al Smith would do in 1960. It is possible he would have voted Republican, but I think he would have prayed Democratic this year."

In this comment, Kennedy not only needled Nixon about his appearance during their debates but also put a plug in for

Democrat Hubert Humphrey, an excellent wit in his own right.

"This week I had the opportunity to debate with Mr. Nixon. I feel that I should reveal that I had a great advantage in that debate, and I am not referring to anyone's makeup man. The advantage that I had was that Mr. Nixon had just debated with Khrushchev, and I had debated with Hubert Humphrey and that gave me an edge."

One of the major Republican campaign issues was that Mr. Kennedy lacked the experience necessary for the presidency. Kennedy had this to say about that criticism in a political speech in Minneapolis in October:

"Ladies and gentlemen, the outstanding news story of this week was not the events of the United Nations or even the presidential campaign. It was a story coming out of my own city of Boston that Ted Williams of the Boston Red Sox had retired from baseball. It seems that at forty-two he was too old. It shows that perhaps experience isn't enough."

Here, during a speech in Norristown, Pennsylvania, Kennedy made fun of Alfred Landon, the Republican who lost to FDR in a 1936 landslide:

"I was informed when I started out this morning that we were going to travel in Delaware County, which voted eight to one for Alf Landon. We are going to wipe that record out. No county in the United States should have that reputation."

During his presidency, Eisenhower was often taken to task for playing golf and generally taking too much time off from his work as chief executive:

"This isn't the way they told me it was when I first decided to run for the presidency," said Kennedy. "After reading about the schedules of the president [Eisenhower], I thought we all stayed in bed until ten or eleven and then got out and drove around."

In Muskegon, Michigan, Kennedy said:

"I want to express my appreciation to the governor. Every time he introduces me as the Potentially Greatest President in the History of the United States, I always think perhaps he is overstating it one or two degrees. George Washington wasn't a bad president and I do not want to say a word for Thomas Jefferson. But, otherwise, I will accept the compliment."

During the campaign, Nixon was hospitalized for a knee injury. Here's how Kennedy responded to a question posed by a reporter.

QUESTION: Senator, when does the moratorium end on Nixon's hospitalization and your ability to attack him?

KENNEDY: Well, I said I would not mention him unless I could praise him until he got out of the hospital, and I have not mentioned him.

Kennedy possessed charm and charisma, and many women thought him handsome. In this comment he was not politically correct by today's standards.

"When I came to Washington to the U.S. Senate, I brought a number of young ladies from Massachusetts to be secretaries. They all got married. Then I got a whole new set of girls and they got married. So if any of you girls feel the prospects are limited in this community, you come and work for me."

LOCAL COLOR

"I am working for the time when unqualified blacks, browns, and women join the unqualified men in running the government."
—*Sissy Farenthold, Texas state representative*

"The biggest danger is for a politician to shake hands with a man who is physically stronger, has been drinking, and is voting for the other guy."
—*William Proxmire, senator from Wisconsin from 1957 to 1989*

Commenting again on his trip to Alaska, Kennedy said:
"I am the first candidate for the presidency to actively campaign in the State of Alaska. There are three electoral votes in Alaska. I left Washington, D.C., this morning at eight o'clock. I have come, I figure, about three thousand miles per electoral vote. And if I travel eight hundred thousand miles in the next two months, we might win this election."

Before the presidential campaign itself, the primaries were tough, and no primary was more critical than West Virginia. To win it, Kennedy campaigned among coal miners—going underground to meet them. One particular miner played into the candidate's plan not to come off like a rich kid who was out of touch with the working class. Some observers suggest that the miner was a plant by the Kennedy team.

"Is it true you're the son of one of our wealthiest men?" one of the miners asked.

Kennedy said it was true.

"Is it true that you've never wanted for anything and had everything you wanted?" he was asked.

"I guess so."

"Is it true you've never done a day's work with your hands all your life?" Kennedy nodded, somewhat hesitantly.

"Well," said the miner, "let me tell you this: You haven't missed a thing."

During his early political years, Kennedy ran for Congress from Boston's tough Eleventh District. He told the story, reportedly true, about the early days of the Irish in Boston. It dealt with a ward boss named Martin Lomasney of the powerful Hendricks Club. People liked this story because it poked fun at the immigrant experience, which many Americans could appreciate.

"It seems that a man named Finnegan moved into Marty Lomasney's ward and after a very short time walked right up to Lomasney and asked if he could be an officer in the Hendricks Club. Lomasney liked his spirit and agreed. Then Finnegan asked if Lomasney would back him to the Common Council. Lomasney was a little surprised, but he did, and of course Finnegan won. Then Finnegan asked if he could have Lomasney's backing for the Great and General Court [State Legislature], and though slightly annoyed, Lomasney gave it to him. Next Finnegan pestered Lomasney for a seat in the State Senate. But still he wasn't satisfied. He came back to Lomasney. 'And what on earth is it you want this time?' Marty asked.

"Please, Mr. Lomasney,' said the new state senator, 'will you help me get my citizenship papers?'"

Here, Kennedy blasts Nixon's poor decision-making powers and his manliness:

"They say Nixon has traveled abroad. He has. In Vietnam he urged the French to continue to fight. On Formosa he implied our support of an invasion of the mainland of China. In India he questioned Nehru's right to be neutral. In Venezuela his goodwill tour evoked a riot, and in the Soviet Union he argued with Mr. Khrushchev in the kitchen, pointing out that while we may be behind in space, we were ahead in color television. Mr. Nixon may be very experienced in kitchen debate; so are a great many other married men I know."

In calling Kennedy another Truman, Nixon thought he would hurt the candidate. Instead, Kennedy turned it around to his advantage.

"Mr. Nixon the other night in my own town of Boston, speaking to his party, said I was another Truman. I regard this as a compliment. And I said he was another Dewey, which he did not regard as a compliment."

In New York City, Kennedy countered Republican claims that the Democrats were soft on defense, wanting to close military factories.

"To show how desperate and despicable [the] campaign has become, they're outside defense plants handing out a poster which says JACK KENNEDY IS AFTER YOUR JOB. I'm after Mr. Eisenhower's job."

Kennedy's campaign team made much of his heroism during World War II, when his boat, *PT109*, was sunk by enemy submarines. Kennedy himself purposely played it down, giving it the opposite effect. When a teenager in Ashland, Wisconsin, asked how he became a hero, Kennedy responded:

"It was involuntary. They sank my boat."

Ohio has always been a prize for candidates because of its large number of electoral votes. Here, Kennedy makes light of campaigning in Ohio.

"There is no city in the United States in which I get a warmer welcome and fewer votes than Columbus, Ohio."

Kennedy did not always receive enthusiastic support from business groups. In February 1961, after the election, Kennedy told the National Industrial Conference Board in Washington: "It would be premature to ask for your support in the next election, and it would be inaccurate to thank you for it in the past."

At a primary stop in Oregon, two young women presented Kennedy with a toy donkey for his daughter.

Kennedy said: "Caroline has the greatest collection of donkeys. She doesn't even know what an elephant looks like. We are going to protect her from that knowledge."

After being president for a short time, Kennedy said:

"When we got into office, the thing that surprised me most was to find that things were just as bad as we'd been saying they were."

Even Adlai Stevenson chimed in on this suggested slogan for Richard Nixon's campaign:

"Don't change administrations in these perilous times into which we have led you."

Many people did not realize that Nixon was a Quaker. He explained his religious background with the following quip:

"My father was a Methodist, my mother was a Quaker. They got married and compromised and my father became a Quaker too."

Eisenhower was an avid golfer, but Nixon was not. When asked by a reporter why he had never seen the candidate play golf, Nixon responded:

"Your comment . . . is probably the most objective comment about the quality of my golf that I've ever heard."

Nixon discussed "mudslinging," which became a part of the 1960 campaign. He said:

"I expect attacks in campaigns. One has been made upon

me of which I have to take some recognition at this dinner. It was not made tonight but made previously. I hesitate to do it. It is of such a serious nature, however, that I think before this particular audience what I consider to be one of the worst smears in American political history has got to be nailed. I read it just a few days ago in the paper. . . . Dateline, Havana. Fidel Castro said, 'The two men running for president of the United States are a couple of beardless youths.'

"Now, I resent that. I resent it because . . . after my first television debate, my makeup man said I had the worst beard since Sal Maglie." (Maglie was a pitcher known as "Sal the Barber," because he gave "close shaves"—that is, pitched very close to hitters. Sal often had a five-o'-clock shadow.)

Nixon was a tough competitor and wasn't afraid to admit it.

"You don't win campaigns with a diet of dishwater and milk toast."

Also . . .

"I have never had much sympathy for the point of view 'It isn't whether you win or lose that counts, but how you play the game.' How you play the game does count. But one must put top consideration on the will, the desire, and the determination to win."

Following his narrow loss to Kennedy, Nixon was able to keep his sense of humor.

In an interview, he described himself as "a dropout from

the electoral college," who had unintentionally "flunked debating."

During the Wisconsin presidential primary, the Kennedy family, including Bobby, Ted, and often their mother and sisters,
went along to help Jack campaign. They would make speeches,
shake hands, and generally support their relative. Hubert
Humphrey, who later lost the nomination to Kennedy, said:

"I feel like an independent merchant competing against
a chain store."

After being defeated by Kennedy in the 1960 West Virginia
primary, Humphrey noted that he had done fairly well for a
Protestant.

He said: "It isn't impossible for a little man to defeat a
big man. After all, David slew Goliath. Of course, what was
sufficiently unusual was that three thousand years later people
are still talking about it."

LOCAL COLOR

"Do I have a great vision to make Louisiana the best
state in the country? I don't know."
—*Jay Blossman, during the 2003 Louisiana governor's race*

"This is the first Convention of the space age—where a
candidate can promise the moon and mean it."
—*NBC News commentator David Brinkley*

Trying to take the wind out of the Democrats' sails, Nixon said:

"The Dodgers might take it all this year. However, there are other events to be held here, of which I am aware. The 1960 Democratic Convention will be held here [Los Angeles], and it may turn out to be the battle of the century."

At the University of North Dakota, Nixon said:

"I want you to know, too, how much I have been moved by the introduction that Governor Davis gave a moment ago. As a matter of fact I was listening over there by the door, and my reaction was that after that introduction, I might as well not make a speech; he had done very well by me already."

On the rigorous schedule of campaigning, Nixon opined:

"We're going over to Council Bluffs from here for another breakfast meeting. The only trouble is we have these breakfast meetings and we never get to eat. The only trouble is we don't get to sleep, because last night we got in at one thirty at night, a wonderful crowd at the airport, and of course had to get up reasonably early this morning. Somebody asked me, 'When do you sleep?' And I decided we're going to take every Thursday off to sleep from now on throughout this campaign."

This story may be apocryphal, but it makes for an amusing tale told by Nixon:

"As a matter of fact, I met a young fellow over in Omaha the other day and you know what he said? 'Will you make me one promise, Mr. Vice President?' And I said, 'Well, I don't know—what is it?' And he said, 'Will you be for a four-day week for school?'"

A campaign promise from Nixon:

"As far as golf is concerned, never having become good enough at it to enjoy it as I should, I think probably I have given it up for the duration; but I've said that before. That's not a campaign promise, I assure you."

In Troy, New York, Nixon told the crowd about a recently tumultuous visit to South America, where people threw stones at the vice president's motorcade:

"And that reminds me, when I went to Caracas, somebody said, 'The vice president got stoned when he was in Caracas.'"

Lyndon Johnson commented to reporters on the vice president's trip with this:

"Son, in politics you've got to learn that overnight, chicken shit can turn to chicken salad."

Campaigning is tough on spouses, Nixon told a crowd:

"In any event I want to say that the wives are tremendously loyal in these campaigns (they have to be). They have to sit there and hear you make that same speech and look as if it's for the first time they ever heard it each time."

A pretty funny story about a confused voter:

"I must share with you one of my favorite recollections of a long hand-shaking session in Florida. We shook hands with over 3,500 people in three hours, and that's moving. But they came through the line and came through the line. Finally one lady came through the line at the last and she looked so tired, because the people had been crowded and jammed in and this lady came through the line and she got up here and said: 'You know, Mr. Nixon, I'm so glad to get here. I didn't think I was going to get here in time to vote for you.'"

On Kennedy supporters, Nixon said:

"I'm glad to see they are here, because we want some people to convert. So we're glad to have you here."

At Fordham University, Nixon noted:

"I happen to be one of those who have received an honorary degree from this institution, and I'm glad to be at least an honorary alumnus. I don't think that I could pass the course today, but I'm glad to get it free.

"It really wasn't entirely free. I had to make a speech."

In Jonestown, Pennsylvania, Nixon came up with this one:

"You know—a funny thing—I really couldn't believe it when somebody said when Mr. Kennedy was here he referred to this place as Johnson City—You know, that's the only time he's mentioned his running mate's name since he has been nominated."

Referring to TV actor James Garner, Nixon told this story:

"Incidentally, as we were coming along, I had a very great compliment paid to me. At least, it will appear that way to my daughters. One of the youngsters alongside of the road said something that Pat overheard. She said, 'You know, he almost looks like Maverick.' "

And another reference to *Maverick*:

"One of the problems people often ask both Pat and me about is: How does running for president or being vice president affect family life?

"Well, you do have a few problems, because sometimes you'll be listening to television and want to tune something in and, you know, the girls may sometimes prefer *Maverick*, and I don't blame them. Sometimes it's better than some of the speeches I have had to listen to."

Nixon went to Whittier College and made these comments about his football career:

"As I look back over here and think of that team and as I see the great stars of that team, I want to tell you something that impresses me. This is the first time these guys have been on the sidelines and I've been on the playing field."

While contemplating a presidential run in 1960, Nixon noted:

"As one who voted for the two-term amendment limiting the holding of the presidency to two terms, I think it would be inconsistent for me to seek the vice presidency for a third term."

One reason for losing the election to Kennedy:

"I was in the Navy in the South Pacific, but I wasn't on a PT boat. That's why I'm here and not in Washington."

After Kennedy won the Democratic nomination, Johnson said:

"Jack was out kissing babies while I was out passing bills. Someone had to tend the store."

Truman made no secret of his disdain for young John F. Kennedy as a prospective Democratic candidate for president in 1960. His opposition had little to do with Kennedy's religion, but much to do with his controversial father. As Truman expressed it: "It's not the Pope I fear but the Pop."

Truman was not a fan of Nixon, either:

"You don't set a fox to watching the chickens just because he has a lot of experience in the henhouse."

Years later, television personality David Frost summed up Nixon's personality problems with this biting observation:

"President Kennedy proved that a man could not be prevented from being president simply because he was a Catholic. Nixon went him one better. He proved that a man could not be prevented from becoming president simply because he was Richard Nixon."

Comedian Mort Sahl was not pleased with either candidate when he said of the election:

"I don't think that either candidate will win."

Richard Harkness, a commentator for the *New York Herald Tribune*, noted:

"When it comes to facing up to serious problems, each

candidate will pledge to appoint a committee. And what is a committee? A group of the unwilling, picked from the unfit, to do the unnecessary. But it all sounds great in a campaign speech."

Caskie Stinnett, travel editor, writer, and humorist, wrote the following in "And If Elected":

"Keep your eye on the candidate who says 'and on the other hand,' because he is arguing both sides of the question and hopes to get you going or coming. A candidate is entitled to work only one side of the street.

"Be especially alert for the candidate who steps out of the parade to shake hands with the legless veteran. You are witnessing theater.

"Look out for the candidate whose American Legion cap fits poorly. He just bought it.

"Avoid the candidate who smiles too much. What's so damned funny?

"Take a second look at the candidate whose voice falters at the end of each page of his speech. He doesn't know, any more than you do, what's coming next.

"When the presidential candidate bestows his blessing upon the local official running for reelection, the rules require the presidential candidate to pronounce correctly the name of his good friend."

On the campaign, author and writer Fletcher Knebel, who was best known for penning the political thriller *Seven Days in May*, offered this "before-and-after" look:

BEFORE:

Nixon theme: "Things are wonderful, and if something isn't done quickly, they'll get even worse."

Kennedy theme: "The country's in such poor shape that even a Democratic administration couldn't hurt it."

Both candidates are leery of corruption charges. In a close election, neither man can take a chance on losing the sinner vote.

AFTER:

Republicans press for vote fraud investigations without fear. They say Nixon was not the type for whom people clamored to vote twice in the same day.

The presidential campaign was loud enough to wake the dead, some of whom turned over in their graves—and mailed in absentee ballots.

Ike appoints Nixon as leader of the Republican Party. That part's easy. Now the trick is to appoint Goldwater and Rockefeller as followers.

Here are some excerpts from writer Robert Bendiner's *How to Listen to Campaign Oratory If You Have To* :

THEY SAY:

My opponent is making a political football out of this grave and complicated issue.

THEY MEAN:

He has a good thing going for him there. If my party was on the paying end of that issue, I'd sure know what to do with it.

THEY SAY:

Let us return to spiritual values.

THEY MEAN:

Let's put my party in again and see what happens.

THEY SAY:

Clean up the mess in Washington.

THEY MEAN:

Clean up their mess in Washington. It will take a few years before we have a mess of our own.

THEY SAY:

We will conduct a vigorous, fighting campaign.

THEY MEAN:

We will smear them.

THEY SAY:

I am not here to make a speech.

THEY MEAN:

I mean to talk for another forty minutes. Don't anyone leave.

THEY SAY:

I am not suggesting that my opponent is personally dishonest.

THEY MEAN:
He is a willing dupe.

THEY SAY:
We will take the American people into our confidence.
THEY MEAN:
We will let them in on all the opposition's scandals we can un-
cover.

THEY SAY:
You may hear talk that they have reformed, my friends, but
the leopard doesn't change its spots.
THEY MEAN:
We haven't been able to get anything new on them lately.

After the election, Nixon was talking to John F. Kennedy's
speechwriter, Ted Sorensen, and said:
"I wish I had said some of those things."
"What part?" asked Sorensen. "The part about 'Ask not
what your country can do for you'?"
"No," Nixon replied. "The part that starts, 'I do solemnly
swear.'"

After his defeat, Nixon remarked:
"We can't all be president—I found that out."

THE ELECTION OF 1964

LYNDON B. JOHNSON, Democrat
43.1 million (486 electoral) Hubert H. Humphrey

BARRY GOLDWATER, Republican
27.2 million (52 electoral) William E. Miller

The election of 1964 will be remembered as a referendum on the civil rights movement as well as for strong opposition to these ideas from a conservative senator from Arizona. It will also be remembered for the very un–politically correct comments of Democrat Lyndon Baines Johnson, a tough pol from Texas who made jokes about illegal immigrants and even his own election scandals. A classic LBJ story focused on his 1948 Senate election, which he won by only an eighty-seven-vote majority. There were allegations of voter fraud in the criminally controlled districts along the Rio Grande. Still, he could joke about the incident even though he was characterized, rather sarcastically, as Landslide Lyndon.

"A man comes upon a child named Pepe in a Texas–Mexico border town and says:

"'What are you crying about, Pepe?'

"'My father came to town yesterday, but didn't come to see me,' said the child.

"'But Pepe, you know your father has been dead for two years.'

"'Yes, but my father came to town to vote for Lyndon Johnson, so why didn't he come to see me?'"

Ouch.

Vice President Johnson took office upon the death of John Kennedy and went on to win a true landslide election against a radically conservative opponent, Barry Goldwater. Even Goldwater had to admit: "We would have lost even if Abraham Lincoln had come back and campaigned with us. Not that he would have campaigned with a right-wing fundamentalist militarist wingnut like me anyway; he'd have probably endorsed Johnson." True enough. Goldwater also was painted by his Democratic opponents as bomb-happy and ready to engage the Soviet Union in an all-out war at the drop of a hat. Toward the end of the campaign, many moderate Republicans refused to back their own party's candidate.

The Arizona senator was perhaps the most conservative Republican candidate since Calvin Coolidge and was more right wing than the Eastern conservative Republican faction led by Nelson Rockefeller and William Scranton. Goldwater was out of step with his own party and most of the nation when he voted against the Civil Rights Act of 1964 that was championed by Johnson. He also characterized Eisenhower's administration as "a dime-store New Deal." Eisenhower's endorsement would have helped Goldwater, but the president appeared in only one ad for his Republican comrade. That in itself was enough for many Republicans to vote against their party's nominee.

Johnson's camp used Goldwater's fringe ideas against him in television ads. One of the most effective, entitled "Daisy Girl," showed a little girl picking daisy petals, with the peaceful scene abruptly shattered by a stark countdown to a nuclear explosion. The ads were a response to Goldwater's call to use nuclear weapons in Vietnam.

The Johnson team also took Goldwater's most important slogan, In Your Heart, You Know He's Right, and changed it to In Your Guts, You Know He's Nuts, a parody that was repeated around office watercoolers for weeks and months.

In contrast, Johnson used extremely catchy slogans, including All the Way with LBJ, and LBJ for the USA.

For their running mates, Johnson was paired with Minnesota senator Hubert Horatio Humphrey, often known as Hubert Horatio Windbag for his long, long speeches.

Goldwater's VP was former congressman William E. Miller, who had been allied with the Dewey camp. He was chairman of the Republican National Committee from 1961 to 1964 but was probably best known after he and Goldwater lost the election and Miller appeared on one of a series of ads for American Express, "Do You Know Me?" These commercials highlighted notable people whose face you might recognize on the street but whose name you couldn't remember.

While Goldwater's defeat was a blow to the Republican Party, his candidacy helped launch the career of Ronald Reagan, who supported Goldwater in a televised speech. Reagan's high profile further moved the Republican base away from their more liberal East Coast brethren and paved the way for Nixon's later comeback as well as Reagan's own election to the presidency. In addition, when Goldwater carried the five Deep South states, it marked the first time that these states voted Republican since the Reconstruction and showed the

GOP that the South could be wrested from Democratic control.

....

In June 1960, after he had announced his intention to seek the Democratic presidential nomination, Johnson toured New Jersey. In one speech, he remarked:

"As I told a friend of Jack's [John F. Kennedy's] last week, we Protestants have proven that we'll vote for a Catholic. Now we want you Catholics to prove that you'll vote for a Protestant."

Johnson liked to tell stories, shaping them to the situation. During the primaries he noted:

"I see in the papers that Barry Goldwater and [Nelson] Rockefeller have decided to cut down their appearances in California. This reminded me of the fellow in Texas who said to his friend, 'Earl, I am thinking of running for sheriff against Uncle Jim Wilson. What do you think?'

"'Well, it depends upon which one of you sees the most people.'

"'That's what I figure.'

"'If you see the most, Uncle Jim will win. If he sees the most, you will win.'"

With all the polls showing Johnson ahead, reporters asked him if there was a problem with him becoming overconfident. He said:

"I don't think it exists. Once, before a very important

election, my wife's car was turned over, and a reporter asked her, 'What was your first thought when you came to?'

"And she said, 'I wish that I had voted absentee.' So we don't believe in overconfidence."

LOCAL COLOR

"What I'm really worried about is what I'm going to do if I'm not elected."
—*Mississippi congressman John Allen, when asked what he would do if he were reelected*

"I also voted for McGovern and Mondale."
—*Actor-comedian Billy Crystal, on his prediction that Michael Spinks would beat Mike Tyson. Tyson knocked out Spinks in less than a minute.*

LBJ talked about the physical dangers of running for office in this story:

"You don't know what suffering is until you have some lady with a great big rough-cut diamond ring just grill it into your finger and squeeze while she tells you her troubles."

After the 1964 Democratic landslide nearly ruined the Republican Party, Johnson studied the election results and said: "I think it's very important that we have a two-party system. I am a fellow that likes small parties, and the Republican Party is about the size I like."

Before the age of political correctness, Johnson told this story to a women's group along the campaign trail:

"Someone brought a big black bulldog into a neighborhood and pretty soon the whole neighborhood was flourishing with little black dogs, very much to the distress of the ladies of the neighborhood. They decided to do something about it, and they consulted a veterinarian.

"They decided to have the dog operated on.

"There was relative calm in the community for about two or three years. Then dogs started flowering again, puppies were waddling down all the sidewalks. And the Ladies Aid Society met and were discussing it, and one old lady said, 'I'll tell you what's happened! It's that damned black bulldog. That's what's causing it all.' And another lady observed, 'Well, I thought we had him operated on.' And the first lady said, 'I know, but he's acting as a consultant.'"

Speechwriter Bob Hardesty wrote this one for Johnson, and he used it to ridicule Republicans:

"There was this old man who needed a heart transplant, and there were three choices in hearts that were available. There was an eighteen-year-old athlete, a nineteen-year-old dancer, and a seventy-five-year-old banker. The patient asked the politics of the banker and was told he was a Republican. Learning this, he chose the banker's heart.

"The transplant was successful, and people asked the

man why he chose the seventy-five-year-old heart instead of those of the vigorous young men. And he said, 'I wanted a heart that I knew had never been used.'"

Johnson did not like Nixon, politically or personally, and the following two comments sum up his feelings. They are also rather prescient, considering what happened during Nixon's presidency:

"I just knew in my heart that it was not right for Dick Nixon to ever be president of this country." He added: "He's like a Spanish horse, who runs faster than anyone for the first nine lengths and then turns around and runs backward. You'll see, he'll do something wrong in the end. He always does."

The Sheraton Park Hotel was crammed with several thousand guests, mostly Texans, and Johnson said: "One thing you can say for the Great Society, it sure is crowded!" Once seated in the presidential box, Johnson spewed one-liners like he was a comedian. For example: "The secretary of labor is in charge of finding you a job," he told guests. "The secretary of the treasury is in charge of taking half of your money away from you, and the attorney general is in charge of suing you for the other half.'"

Adlai Stevenson was asked to introduce Lyndon Johnson at a Washington dinner and said:

"You are doing so well that even the Republicans like you. They can find only two things wrong—your foreign policy and your domestic policy."

Just before the election, Richard Nixon commented on the race that was obviously going to be a landslide for Johnson. Making fun of his own experience, he said:

"[You] should see some of my mail. I received a letter the other day which said, 'The Republicans should nominate you. They're going to lose anyway. Why not choose an expert in losing?' "

In a bit a self-deprecating humor, Nixon noted just before the election:

"I promised Lyndon that I'll get him the fellow who made me up for the first debate with Kennedy in Chicago 1960."

Goldwater had a sense of humor about the impending landslide:

"I'm too young to retire and too old to go back to work."

One of Goldwater's favorite stunts during the campaign was to poke his fingers through a pair of lensless black-rimmed glasses (similar to the kind he really wore) and say, "These glasses are just like Lyndon Johnson's programs. They look good, but they don't work."

The Johnson family owned the first television station in Austin. They had also owned radio stations. Goldwater took issue with Johnson's control of Austin's only television outlet in this story:

"I took off from Dallas this morning, but before I did I asked the lieutenant on the line, 'How do you get to Austin?'

"He said, 'Well, you head south and keep flying about an hour and fifteen minutes and then you're going to see a big city with only one television antenna. That's Austin.'"

Michigan governor George Romney was a possible choice for the Republican presidential nomination, and Goldwater made fun of his campaign:

"Governor Romney says he's getting tired of telling people that he's not a candidate for the Republican nomination. What's more, he's getting tired of all the traveling he has to do to tell them."

One day, Barry Goldwater's campaign manager brought him to a restaurant during lunch to shake hands with customers. Goldwater reluctantly complied but said this:

"If somebody walked up to me while I was eating lunch and stuck out his hand, I'd put a hamburger right in his palm."

Although Johnson personally was a frugal man, Goldwater attacked what he believed were Democrats' penchant for overspending. He said:

"The immediate task before us is to cut the federal government down to size. . . . We must take Lyndon's credit card away from him."

Always the hawk, Goldwater told workers at a Boeing bomber plant in Seattle that had been hit by cutbacks, "I guess when the next war comes, defense officials will go to Hertz rent-a-bomber."

Although the Democrats clearly had better campaign slogans, Goldwater came up with this one for his opponent:

"LBJ. That stands for Light Bulb Johnson. Let's turn him out in November."

An exclusive Washington, D.C., organization founded in 1913, the Alfalfa Club, holds an annual banquet to honor the birthday of General Robert E. Lee. At their banquets they "nominate" a presidential candidate (even people who are not in politics), and this person is expected to offer a humorous speech.

In 1962, they "nominated" Goldwater, and here are his comments:

"Emotion chokes me when I think that you have chosen a barefoot boy from the Arizona 'valley of fear' to lead this underprivileged, undernourished, underhoused, underclothed, and over-Kennedied nation of under one hundred and ninety million underlings back to the Old Frontier of McKinley's day. The undertaking, naturally, overwhelms me. It takes my breath away even though I feel the White House is ready for me since Jacqueline remodeled it in an eighteenth-century décor, and I feel this is a double honor, since I've never even been to Harvard. . . .

"Now I must take note of the fact that my opponents call me a conservative. If I understand the word correctly, it means to 'conserve'—Well, then, I'm just trying to live up to my name and conserve two things that most need conserving in this country—gold and water.

"The first plank [of my campaign] fits neatly on one page, but I think it's basically sound and honest. It will mean the same thing to you whether you live in the North or South, whether you're a farmer in Maine or an industrial worker in California. It says, and I ask you to pay close attention: ELECT GOLDWATER. . . . The other two planks deal with labor, education, foreign policy, and the farm problem. Here's Plank Number Two—ELECT GOLDWATER. Now, you may notice a certain similarity between the first plank and the second, and I want you to know that that was deliberate. It has been my experience that the public is confused if you offer too many issues. The thing to do is to get hold of one good one and stick to it. Hammer it home. Repetition is the way Madison Avenue sells toothpaste and soap, and it's the way the New Frontier stays in the limelight. But when repetition occurs at the White House—and it has since 1932—it's not a sales pitch, it's a giveaway. You don't even have to guess the price.

"And now for the final plank—Plank Number Three. This is the bell-ringer, and it's even shorter. It just says DITTO."

He continued:

"Now, I suppose no acceptance speech would be complete without a reference to the candidate's background. Very simply, I think I'm in the American tradition. I was born in a log cabin, which I had moved to Phoenix, and except for some air-conditioning, a swimming pool, a bowling alley, a bar, a shooting range, and a golf course, it remains the simple log cabin it always was.

"I have nothing against millionaire presidents. I'd just like to see the day return when people other than presidents can be millionaires too.

"I've never hesitated with an answer. When anyone asks me how I stand on integration, I've only got one answer—Where are you from?

"Now, gentlemen, I have told you the story. The rest is up to you. Go out and work from now to election day and fulfill our campaign pledge—ELECT GOLDWATER. Find more of those districts such as the one the New Frontier turned up in Cook County—the one that had twenty-two residents but came up with seventy-seven votes. That's the sort of stuff I mean.

"Gentlemen, I'm flattered that you thought first of my name. I have every confidence that with all of you behind me, I could be another Alf Landon."

LOCAL COLOR

"Anyone can be elected once by accident, but with the second term, it's worth paying attention."
—*Legendary Speaker of the House of Representatives
Sam Rayburn*

"A Troubled Man for Troubled Times."
—*Campaign slogan of rocker Alice Cooper during his run for
Arizona governor*

Goldwater made light of Humphrey's ability to deliver speeches rapidly:

"Hubert Humphrey talks so fast that listening to him is like trying to read *Playboy* magazine with your wife turning over the pages."

After the election, Goldwater quipped:
"It's a great country, where anybody can grow up to be president . . . except me."

In 1996, Goldwater told Bob Dole, who also mounted his presidential campaign with lukewarm support from hardline conservatives, "We're the new liberals of the Republican Party. Can you imagine that?"

Vice-presidential candidate William Miller often played bridge with reporters while touring the country—and he usually won. Finally, one reporter asked him if he would give him a chance to get even by betting on the outcome of the election. Miller said that he might seem stupid, but he wasn't crazy enough to bet on the outcome of this election.

Humphrey was growing weary of politicking but kept his sense of humor:
"When I got home one night after four television programs, I opened the refrigerator door to get something to eat. When the light went on, I gave a ten-minute speech to a head of lettuce."

The following story that Humphrey told may be apocryphal, but it's funny nonetheless. He recounted when

Johnson telephoned to ask him if he would be his running mate:

"Hubert, do you think you can keep your mouth shut for the next four years?"

"Yes," Humphrey said.

"There you go interrupting me again!" yelled LBJ.

Goldwater said of Humphrey's long-windedness:

"Hubert has been clocked at 275 words a minute, with gusts up to 340."

As to the fact that Humphrey was long-winded, his wife, Muriel, told her husband, "Hubert, a speech, to be immortal, doesn't have to be eternal."

In 1966, two years after the election, Humphrey told the Gridiron Club Dinner:

"As most of you remember, it was a very clean campaign, without the usual name-calling that goes with a presidential election. To this day, I have a great deal of respect for Barry Goldwater and his running mate, what's-his-name."

In August, during the anxious period just before Johnson announced his choice for vice president, Humphrey was on pins and needles waiting for word. Three days before the decision deadline, a television reporter asked Humphrey if he was nervous, but it was clear that the reporter was on edge too:

"Senator, do you know anything? Are you nervous? Are you anxious? How are you holding up?"

"Obviously a lot better than you are," Humphrey replied calmly.

In his ironic way, Humphrey commented on his decision to accept the vice-presidential nomination. He could not articulate exactly what he was bringing to the ticket but said:

"I weighed the decision on the vice presidency very carefully. Not long, but carefully . . . I didn't have . . . reluctance!"

Humphrey told a group of student supporters of Barry Goldwater during the campaign, "I don't care if you study ancient history, but don't vote for it."

Being chosen to run for vice president required a lot of tact, being in the right place at the right time, and hanging out with the right people. Humphrey joked about this in the following:

"Just look at what's happened. The president sent Bobby Kennedy to the Far East. He sent Sargent Shriver to deliver a message to the Pope. Adlai Stevenson got to escort Mrs. Johnson when she went to the theater in New York. So I asked the president, 'Who's going to enroll [your daughter] Lynda Bird in George Washington University? I'll volunteer.'"

Johnson had some misgivings that Humphrey might upstage him. The vice-presidential candidate allayed his fears by saying:

"That's like Rembrandt worrying about a college art student."

President Johnson kept everyone guessing about his choice for vice president until the last minute. Humphrey was on the short list, but Johnson enjoyed stringing him along. Humphrey described it this way:

"He discussed every move and thought with me as if nothing could interest me less personally. It's like a guy calling the girl next door—who he knows is madly in love with him—to ask the phone number of the newest broad in town."

Goldwater's negative attitude was not lost on the voters or Humphrey, who said:

"And where was Senator Goldwater? He was under the no-no tree in the shadow of his own indifference."

Just before the election, in response to Barry Goldwater's accusing President Johnson of "daddyism" (so called because Johnson often got his way through bullying), Humphrey defended his running mate by saying of Goldwater:

"He's against Daddy, against labor, and against old people and young people. And there's still time for him to say something against Mother."

In November, just before the election, Miller kidded Humphrey about his middle name.

Humphrey responded: "I think America is entitled to a vice president with the middle name of Horatio."

Reporters repeatedly asked Robert Kennedy whether he was willing to be Lyndon Johnson's running mate.

REPORTER: How do you feel about a Johnson–Kennedy ticket?

KENNEDY: I'd be willing, but I'm not sure that Mr. Johnson would accept the vice presidency.

Jimmy Carter's son Chip wore an LBJ button to school one day, and some classmates who did not like Johnson ripped it off. The next day he wore the button and again it was torn off. This continued for several days until finally a gang of bigger and older boys roughed him up so badly that Chip went home in tears. "Put the button back on," his father ordered. "What if they tear it off again?" asked Chip. "Put it on again," said Carter. "Then," said Chip, "they'll just tear it off again." "Then," said Carter, "you just put it back on again, if you want to wear it. Do what you want to do—and then learn to box."

·During the campaign, Johnson reportedly discharged one of his political "advance men" for making a pass at a young woman who was a member of the staff. A farewell party was held for the man, during which Press Secretary Bill Moyers presented him with a picture of the president, autographed by Moyers and bearing the following inscription: "To_____, who made one advance too many."

THE ELECTION OF 1968

RICHARD M. NIXON, Republican
31.8 million (301 electoral) Spiro T. Agnew

HUBERT H. HUMPHREY, Democrat
31.3 million (191 electoral) Edmund S. Muskie

GEORGE C. WALLACE, American Independent
9.9 million (46 electoral) Curtis F. Lemay

How many presidential candidates would be willing to go on one of the most popular TV shows, stick his head through a door, and yell "Sock it to me!"? As if the country's tenor was not wild enough, candidate Nixon appeared on the hit comedy show *Laugh-In*, which featured the recurring catchphrase followed by a water dousing or a bonk over the head with a pillow or vaudeville-type rubber bladder. Richard Nixon's somewhat stiff rendition of the catchphrase was parodied by comedians for years following the appearance, and it helped him moderate some of the rigidity that many voters found undesirable in the Republican candidate. Humphrey declined the same invitation and later said that not appearing may have cost him the election.

This was one of the more amusing moments during the tumultuous 1968 campaign. The country was in turmoil, roiled by race riots that erupted in dozens of cities, antiwar marches in Washington, the assassinations of Robert Kennedy and Martin Luther King Jr., and a general feeling among voters that the country was heading in the wrong direction.

For the Democrats, it was particularly tough because their party was being blamed for the Vietnam quagmire and the "liberal" attitude that had brought lawlessness to the nation.

No Democrat was willing to run against Johnson, the sitting president—at first—but antiwar activist Eugene McCarthy and later Robert Kennedy (who was assassinated shortly after announcing his bid) did make a run on Johnson's presidency. In March, however, Johnson decided not to run, leaving the party in disarray. Eventually, Hubert Humphrey was nominated by Democrats and had the impossible task of trying to shed the Vietnam War legacy left by Johnson as well as the television coverage of beatings of protestors by Chicago police during the Democratic convention. By association, voters increasingly blamed Democrats for the chaos they saw at home and in Southeast Asia.

The Republicans nominated Richard Nixon after his main competitor, Michigan governor George Romney, said that he had been "brainwashed" by the military into supporting the Vietnam War. Labeled as a nutcase, Romney ceased to be a factor. Nelson Rockefeller and Ronald Reagan made late bids against Nixon but were unsuccessful.

For their running mates, Nixon chose Maryland governor Spiro T. ("Spiro Who?") Agnew, and Humphrey's election partner was former Maine governor and senator Edmund S. Muskie. Agnew will be remembered for many campaign misspeaks' including, "To one extent, if you've seen one city slum, you've seen them all."

After having lost the 1960 election to Kennedy and a 1962 governor's race in California, Nixon would be labeled the "comeback kid"—recognition that Nixon had pulled himself back up to become a national political force. Nixon told voters that he had a secret plan (he didn't have one) to end the Vietnam War and would address disorder in the streets by choosing a tough U.S. attorney general who would bring law and order to the nation.

Also entering the mix was Alabama governor George Wallace of the American Independent Party. At first he was dismissed, but he proved to be a formidable candidate despite his blatantly racist platform. His initial constituency was whites who wanted to roll back civil rights laws that gave blacks equal footing, but as the election day neared, he also appealed to those who disliked the Supreme Court's "liberal" decisions such as federal interference in local schools (and other states' rights issues) and, as Wallace put it, those "left-wingers in both national parties who have brought us to the domestic mess we are in now."

In the end, Nixon prevailed, but Wallace received almost ten million votes and carried the Southern states of Arkansas, Mississippi, Georgia, Alabama, and Louisiana. In the electoral college, Nixon got 301 votes, Humphrey 191, and Wallace received 46 (in addition to the five aforementioned states, he got one vote from North Carolina)—an amazing feat for a third-party candidate.

In many ways, the election of 1968 will be remembered not only for the humor generated by its candidates but by jokes generated by the media, Yippies, Hippies, and the general public who saw little to praise in either of the two major candidates and just wanted the whole mess to be over. Humor became a way of coping with a very anxious and tense time.

When a reporter queried people in downtown Atlanta about who Spiro Agnew was, the response was hysterical:

"I'm going to mention two words to you. You tell me what they mean. The words are: Spiro Agnew."

One man replied, "It's some kind of disease." Another said, "It's some kind of egg." A third responded, "He's a Greek who owns that shipbuilding firm."

Even Agnew himself was candid about it. "Spiro Agnew," he admitted, "is not a household word."

During a campaign meeting in Syracuse, New York, Nixon summed up his thoughts on the nation and the upcoming election:

"There is nothing wrong with this country that a good election can't fix."

LOCAL COLOR

"Half of the American people have never read a newspaper. Half never voted for president. One hopes it is the same half."
—*Author Gore Vidal*

"Eight more days, and I can start telling the truth again."
—*Connecticut senator Christopher Dodd's joke on campaigning*

When asked about poverty, Agnew said:

"You don't learn from people suffering from poverty but from experts who have studied the problem."

As Agnew's missteps accrued, he found himself greeted by the following poster at one rally: APOLOGIZE NOW, SPIRO. IT WILL SAVE TIME.

Johnson invited Humphrey to the LBJ ranch to discuss the campaign. While they were walking and talking, Johnson moved the discussion to a cow pasture, where Humphrey immediately stepped in a pile of manure. "Mr. President," said Humphrey as soon as he regained his equanimity, "I just stepped on the Republican platform!"

Humphrey stepped off a plane in Fargo, North Dakota, to speak before a huge crowd. He walked down the ramp and said:

"I couldn't believe my eyes when I saw this huge crowd so late at night. For a moment I felt like a Republican; I thought I was walking in my sleep."

During the campaign, Humphrey often found himself heck-led by hostile people in crowds, and he became somewhat flus-tered. Nixon, on the other hand, always seemed composed and tranquil, especially on television ads. Humphrey decided to show crowds his passion compared to what he considered to be Nixon's quiet, sometimes callous demeanor.

Discussing this matter, he said:

"You know, every day I read about that cool, that confident, that composed and that smiling Mr. Nixon—the man who campaigns without running, the man who takes it easy and never makes a mistake . . . who either evades or straddles every issue. I'm going to send Mr. Nixon some talcum powder. He must be getting saddle sores, straddling all those issues."

Perhaps the worst understatement of the campaign was uttered by Agnew when he said of self-proclaimed racist Strom Thurmond:

"Senator Thurmond hasn't been as interested in achieving some aims of the black community as civil rights leaders."

When asked if he encountered any animosity while campaigning in the African American community, Agnew noted:

"I haven't encountered any hostility from Negro citizens as I move around. . . . If you just walk out on the street, you get just as much of a fine reception from Negroes as you get from any other citizens."

In a campaign speech at Madison Square Garden, George Wallace complained that the media made him look bad on purpose. Here's what he had to say:

"Well now, all you television folks get a good picture over there now. Go ahead. You know—now it's all over. Get this camera turned back this way. You know—everywhere we've spoken we've had this same kind of crowd, but the television puts all this footage on a few folks that don't know how to

NIXON vs. HUMPHREY | 99

behave in a crowd and make it appear that there are no people supporting you here. And I frankly think the networks are doing that on purpose. Myself, I don't think they want to show the support we have here in New York City and throughout the country. Yes sir, but I think they know to-night and have seen something they didn't expect in Madison Square Garden, and I reckon they'll try to explain it away to-morrow, *The New York Times* and the other papers will. But you just remember that some of these newspapers can fool some of the people some of the time, but they can't fool all the people all the time. You remember that."

Wallace also complained about people's manners, having been the brunt of heckling and booing almost everywhere he spoke:

"The liberals and the left-wingers in both national par-ties have brought us to the domestic mess we are in now. And also this foreign mess we are in . . . [there is shouting and hissing in the crowd] You need to read the book *How to Behave in a Crowd*. You really don't know how to behave in a crowd, do you? Yes, the liberals and left-wingers in both parties have brought us to the domestic mess we are in, also to the foreign policy mess we find our nation involved in at the present time, personified by the no-win war in Southeast Asia."

Later, Wallace was distracted and then confused by the appearance of someone in the audience:

"Well, I want to tell Mr. Nixon it's a good thing he doesn't debate, because if he ever does, we're going to point out that he's made so many inconsistent statements about so many matters, I would be happy to debate. But he cannot get a debate started.

"That's all right. That's all right, honey—that's right sweetie-pie—oh, that's a he, I thought you were a she, I tell you what, I got . . ."

Agnew's unintentional humor continued to be a mainstay of the presidential election. In this instance, asked how he would help the president fulfill his duties, Agnew said:

"I think I could take some of the burdens off the president in the way of entertaining visitors."

Agnew responded to a question about his public image in this way:

"My public image isn't the greatest thing I've ever seen."

About two months before the election, Agnew said this:

"People are getting too edgy when they take umbrage at being called Polacks and Japs."

While he was House Minority Leader, Gerald Ford critiqued the Republican contenders:

"Nelson [Rockefeller] is the best man to save the American dollar. It's a family habit. . . . Rockefeller is the only taxpayer who can balance the federal budget with his mad money.

"Dick Nixon doesn't have to stay in politics for the money. Only last week the Schick Razor Company offered him two million dollars just to do a shaving commercial . . . for Gillette. . . . Dick is the only candidate who gets five-o'-clock shadow on the *Today* show."

Reagan's supporters began pushing him for the presidency as early as 1968, but he held back:

"It would be presumptuous of me to say I should run after two years as governor," he told them.

"If you think you're not up to it," said one of them impatiently, "tell us."

"No," said Reagan. "I feel I'm better qualified to be president than governor."

He did not announce his availability until a few hours before the first ballot, and Richard Nixon easily won the nomination that year.

Discussing his misspeaks, Agnew promised voters:

"I have often been accused of putting my foot in my mouth, but I will never put my hand in your pockets."

Bud Wilkinson, football player, coach, and broadcaster, asked Nixon:

"As a football coach, occasionally we'd be ahead at halftime, and I'd go in there wondering, How about the complacency factor? All the polls and consensus say you are ahead. How do you feel about that?"

Nixon responded: "I've watched your teams. I have seen them play in the Orange Bowl. You were a great third-quarter team—not first half, but the third quarter.

"By the time you got through with the third quarter, the fourth quarter didn't matter.

"Now, we are just entering the third quarter of this campaign. I am going to remember what you did. We are going to roll it up right now, and as far as complacency is concerned, people say, 'Well, it's going to be like Dewey in 1948,' and somebody has said that Humphrey is going to come back like Truman did.

"Well, I just don't believe it, because a lot of things are different. I think it's one thing to give them hell, but it's something else to give them Humphrey."

Discussing the Nixon–Agnew platform, Agnew said, ironically as it turned out:

"A Nixon–Agnew administration will abolish the credibility gap and reestablish the truth—the whole truth—as its policy."

After winning the election, Nixon said:

"Having lost a close one eight years ago, and having won a close one this year, I know winning is a lot more fun."

Said Nixon of the turmoil within the Democratic Party during a time in which hippies were "dropping out" of society:

"With George Romney, Nelson Rockefeller, and Lyndon Johnson all bowing out of the fight, it was beginning to look like the year of the dropout."

Nixon noted:

"I have said on several occasions, sometimes facetiously, sometimes seriously, that I know what it means to be nominated; now I want to get elected."

Nixon was well aware of his physical characteristics when he spoke to a meeting of editorial cartoonists:

"Now, I'm not speaking of my editorial views; we might disagree on that. But just think of the fun you would have for four years, drawing me. Now, look what your loss was, when you lost Lyndon Johnson. That great face—you know, with the big ears and the big nose, and look at my nose: I can do even better than Johnson, as far as that's concerned."

To the B'nai B'rith Convention, Nixon said:

"When I used to address organizations like this in years like this, I often used to say after the election in 1960 that I only wish I had been a member of an organization in which the vice president automatically became president. I can't say that tonight—not that I am prejudiced, of course. I just simply want to say that I have been trying to figure a way that I could get one up on my good friend Mr. Humphrey, and it occurred to me that both of us have served in the United States Senate. We are, therefore, highly aware of the rules of seniority. It is true that both of us have also served as vice president, but he has been vice president only four years; I was vice president eight years. I have seniority. And so I think it is my turn."

Once, Nixon was accidentally called Hubert Humphrey, and he said:

"Now, I'm not particularly sensitive. I've been called almost everything. But please don't call me Hubert."

During the New Hampshire primary, Nixon told reporters:

"Ladies and gentlemen, as we start this campaign there's one thing we should say at the outset—this is not my last press conference."

LOCAL COLOR

"Come pretty near having two holidays of equal importance in the same week—Halloween and election. And of the two, election provides us the most fun. On Halloween they put pumpkins on their heads, and on election they don't have to."
—*Humorist Will Rogers*

"For a candidate to spend millions of dollars during the primaries to win a job that pays only $100,000 a year, doesn't bode well for the citizens' hopes of electing a man to this high office whose knowledge of economics will balance our national budget."
—*Columnist Goodman Ace*

Speaking to a crowd, Nixon quipped:
"I always like to see college kids. I'm trying to get into a college this year myself—the electoral college."

To a dinner audience, Nixon said:
"Go ahead and finish your dessert—at these Johnson prices, it may be your last meal."

Referring to the incident in which North Korea killed one crew member and held hostage other crew members of the USS *Pueblo* for eighteen months, Nixon said:

"What stimulates you, what keeps you going, believe it or not are those crowds you see out there. They are not all for us, and some of them carry signs for other candidates. I saw one the other day that said TRADE HUBERT FOR THE PUEBLO. I don't think North Korea would take him."

Making light of having been the vice president but never the president, Nixon joked:

"And so I do have an announcement to make today. Today will duly record I shall not seek, and I shall not accept my party's nomination for, vice president of the United States."

When asked if his running for president would split the Democratic Party, Eugene McCarthy stated:

"Have you ever tried to split sawdust?"

Speaking to a meeting of editorial cartoonists, Nixon noted:

"And then one of the friendly reporters asked about the new Nixon, and I was beginning to swell up and I think, Well, gee, there really is a 'New Nixon,' and I was just feeling I really had a chance this year. Next day, I saw a Herblock cartoon—the same OLD Nixon."

To an audience in Oregon, Nixon told how he and Nelson Rockefeller lived in the same Manhattan apartment building, and he was hoping for a new place:

"Mrs. Nixon and I decided we don't like an apartment too well. We think maybe next year we'd like to move into a house—if you'll help us."

Making fun of Humphrey's penchant for long speeches, Nixon said:

"In fact, my friends, it appears that the great debate this year is going to be Humphrey versus Humphrey, and I'm going to have to ask for equal time."

Pumping up the crowd, Nixon stated:

"The voters of Oregon have spoken, and I like the sound of their voices."

A jab at the Johnson family wealth, Nixon said:

"Lyndon Johnson served in the House, the Senate, and as vice president. I served in the House, the Senate, and as vice president. Lyndon Johnson has a dog. I have a dog. Lyndon has two daughters. I have two daughters. Lyndon Johnson has a lovely wife. I have a lovely wife. Lyndon Johnson has a television station. . . .

"I have a lovely wife."

Ronald Reagan responded to the possibility that he would be offered the vice presidency in '68 in this way:

"There is absolutely no circumstance whatever under which I would accept that spot. Even if they tied and gagged me, I would find a way to signal by wiggling my ears."

During the campaign, Nixon often invoked the name of Eisenhower because he was a popular president. In Portland, Oregon he introduced Ike's son:

"And this is David Eisenhower. I always run better with an Eisenhower."

When Nixon announced that Agnew was his choice for vice president, the news media and the public said "Spiro Agnew—Who's He?" leading one commentator to note that the name rhymed with either "hero" or "zero."

Describing the long shot that was Barry Goldwater, the *Seattle Post-Intelligencer* declared: "It may be that Barry Goldwater will be elected. That Chase National will go broke, that Governor Wallace will get an honorary degree from Tuskegee, and that Mickey Spillane will win the Nobel Prize for Literature."

Journalist and muckraker I. F. Stone noted after what he called the GOP's "Nixonian cheerfest" in Miami Beach in 1968:

"It was hard to listen to Goldwater and realize that a man could be half Jewish and yet sometimes appear to be twice as dense as the normal gentile. As for Agnew, even at a convention where every speech seemed to outdo the other in wholesome clichés and delicious anticlimaxes, his speech putting Nixon into nomination topped all the rest. If the race that produced Isaiah is down to Goldwater and the race that produced Pericles is down to Agnew, the time has come to give the country back to the WASPs."

THE ELECTION OF 1972

RICHARD M. NIXON, Republican
47.2 million (520 electoral) Spiro T. Agnew

GEORGE McGOVERN, Democrat
29.2 million (17 electoral) Sargent Shriver

JOHN G. SCHMITZ, American
1.1 million (0 electoral) Thomas J. Anderson

George McGovern summed up the election perfectly when he said, "Three things beat me. Dirty tricks, tapped phones . . . and I lost forty-nine states." The loss was not unexpected. When Democrat McGovern gave his acceptance speech at the party's convention held in Miami Beach, it was 2:48 a.m. and fewer than four million television viewers stayed up to watch. This was a bad sign of things to come for the donkey party as it worked through convention disruptions from differing minority factions—each demanding voting quotas for their delegates. At times, there was so much anger and confusion among delegates that votes were scattered among seventy candidates, including throwaway nods to TV reporter Roger Mudd and China's Chairman Mao Zedong.

McGovern's chances weren't helped when it was discovered that his vice-presidential candidate, Missouri senator Thomas Eagleton, had undergone electroshock therapy for depression—information that had been kept from McGovern. At first, McGovern promised to back Eagleton "1,000 percent," but days later asked him to resign. Kennedy family member Sargent Shriver replaced him. The late-night comics and columnists had a field day. Humorist Art Buchwald said of the Democratic candidate, "I thought McGovern would be hopeless from a humor standpoint, but he fooled me. The minute that he backed Eagleton 1,000 percent, I knew I was home free."

For the Republicans, the choice was obvious: President Richard Nixon and Spiro Agnew.

Nixon had finally become more comfortable with television and was able to reach voters with his message that the Vietnam War was coming to a close. Only weeks before the election he told Americans that "peace was at hand" and closer to the election went on television to declare that "peace with honor" was in the offing. In fact, the United States was drawing down troops but increasing air attacks. Americans were fed up with the war, yet believed Nixon's assessment that a resolution was close at hand even though it was not quite true.

Voters also ignored early newspaper reports about the Watergate break-in in June 1972 and instead focused on the president's opening up of relations with China, which made Nixon appear like a conciliatory chap.

All of this "positive news" seemed like a winner compared with the floundering of the Democrats, and Nixon won the election.

· · · · · · · · ·

After the election, McGovern said:

"For years, I wanted to run for president in the worst possible way, and I'm sure I did."

The 1972 Republican convention in Miami that nominated Richard Nixon and Spiro Agnew had little drama or excitement. Nixon joked defensively about its clear predictability:

"Those people who said that what took place in Miami was unexciting because we knew how it was going to turn out . . . well, I have never seen a John Wayne movie that was unexciting because you knew he was going to get the bad guy in the end."

Agnew may have toned down his inflammatory rhetoric, but he kept firing his acerbic comments—especially at Sargent Shriver, the Democratic vice-presidential candidate. Shriver, John Kennedy's brother-in-law, had his own wealth and that of the Kennedy family to draw on.

Said Agnew: "My opponent says he knows what it means to be poor. He says 'When I was a kid, my father had eight hungry mouths to feed. My mother and me and six polo ponies.'"

Agnew continued with a made-up story about what it would have been like if he and Shriver had been childhood chums:

"I have vivid memories," said Agnew, "of little Sarge when we'd play hide-and-seek. I'd hide and he'd put a private detective on retainer to go out and find me."

McGovern joked about the Watergate bugging when he said the following to the annual Al Smith Charity Dinner in New York:

"I'm sorry President Nixon can't be with us tonight. But I'm sure that somewhere he's listening in."

LOCAL COLOR

"You campaign in poetry, you govern in prose."
—*Mario Cuomo, governor of New York from 1983 to 1995*

"In every election in American history, both parties have their clichés. The party that has the clichés that ring true wins."
—*Notable House Speaker Newt Gingrich*

During his acceptance of his party's nomination McGovern tried to put a happier face on the crumbling Democratic Party.

"Never underestimate the power of Richard Nixon to bring harmony to Democratic ranks."

McGovern appeared to be out of step with the electorate on many issues:

"You know, sometimes, when they say you're ahead of your time, it's just a polite way of saying you have a real bad sense of timing."

After the election, McGovern was able to make light of his loss, saying: "The whole campaign was a tragic case of mistaken identity."

After Eagleton left the campaign and Shriver was named to replace him, Shriver was able to joke about it, saying:

"I am not embarrassed to be George McGovern's seventh choice for vice president. Pity Mr. Nixon; his first and only choice was Spiro Agnew."

During a campaign stop, Shriver told a group of parents how he pushed his children to be better students. He told this story:

"I told them, 'When Lincoln was your age he walked twelve miles to school every day.' But my son said, 'That's nothing. When Uncle Jack was your age, he was president.'"

On the PBS program *America's Political Parties*, House Speaker Tip O'Neill was reminiscing about the election and joked about how McGovern was "nominated by the cast of *Hair*."

Said Art Buchwald:

"I can now reliably report that Vice President Spiro Agnew has no intention of dumping Richard Nixon. A spokesman for the vice president told me that Agnew was very satisfied with the job his president was doing and that he even intended to give him more responsibilities than any vice president has ever given his president before."

Professionally, Buchwald was quite pleased that Nixon was reelected, because it offered many opportunities to make fun of him. Buchwald said: "I worship the quicksand he walks in."

Georgia's Julian Bond said of McGovern's decision to drop Eagleton because he had been treated for mental illness:

"At least we know ours had treatment. What about theirs?"

In this slip of the tongue, Frank Licht, then governor of Rhode Island, said while campaigning for McGovern:

"Nixon has been sitting in the White House while George McGovern has been exposing himself to the people of the United States."

Political writer and gonzo journalist Hunter S. Thompson noted in *Fear and Loathing: On the Campaign Trail '72*: "It was not until his campaign collapsed and his ex-staffers felt free to talk that I learned that working for Big Ed [Muskie, who ran unsuccessfully for vice president with McGovern] was something like being locked in a rolling boxcar with a vicious 200-pound water rat."

THE ELECTION OF 1976

JIMMY CARTER, Democrat
40.8 million (297 electoral) Walter F. Mondale

GERALD FORD, Republican
39.1 million (240 electoral) Robert J. Dole

EUGENE McCARTHY, Independent
756,631 (0 electoral) None

By the time the 1976 election rolled around, Americans were more cynical about their government and politics in general than they had been in years. And, they were ready for a "boring" president, someone who would just get the country through the next few years without scandal, war, or controversy. Good luck with that.

Vice President Gerald Ford had taken over for Nixon after his resignation, and the new president was often portrayed on television comedy shows, such as the very popular *Saturday Night Live*, as a klutz who kept stumbling and falling. This was based on truth; Ford suffered a spate of real life missteps that were covered by the media and played on the nightly news. Ford was able to make light of his lack of coordination and also use humor to deflect criticism of his pardon of Nixon. At one press conference, reporter Fred Barnes asked:

"Mr. President, two or three times today you talked about your 'predecessor.' and once you referred to 'Lyndon Johnson's successor'. Are you trying to avoid saying the name Richard M. Nixon?"

"Yes," said Ford.

The Democrats put forth former Naval officer, submariner, peanut farmer, and all-around straight guy Georgia governor Jimmy Carter. The born-again Christian with the toothy smile appealed to politics-weary voters when he promised, "I will never lie to the American people." He also displayed a sense of humor when he said, "My tax audit is coming out OK. The only thing they questioned so far is a six-hundred-dollar bill for toothpaste."

Carter campaigned hard for the nomination, beating rivals Representative Morris "Mo" Udall of Arizona, former Senator Fred Harris of New Mexico, and former vice-presidential candidate Sargent Shriver.

With the electorate tuned into Ford's physical gaffes, they were also watching for verbal missteps, and the president didn't disappoint the public when he said during a debate with Carter that most of Eastern Europe was not under Soviet control. It was a statement that everyone, even Ford, acknowledged had done great damage, especially after the questioner gave Ford the opportunity to correct his mistake and Ford dug himself even deeper (see the excerpt below).

Still, the final election outcome was close (with one electoral vote from Washington going to Ronald Reagan).

Although he ran under no party designation, Senator Eugene McCarthy received almost 757,000 popular votes (no electoral votes), but he is notable because he fought restrictive election laws state-by-state, which helped pave the way for future third-party candidates to get on the ballot.

· · · · · · · · · ·

Of his opponent in the primaries, Ford said:

"Ronald Reagan doesn't dye his hair; he's just prematurely orange."

Again, referring to Reagan, Ford said: "Governor Reagan and I do have one thing in common. We both played football. I played in Michigan. He played for Warner Brothers."

Here is Ford's famous debate misspeak:

"There is no Soviet domination of Eastern Europe, and there never will be under a Ford administration."

New York Times reporter Max Frankel offered Ford the chance to take back this obvious mistake, but it got worse.

Frankel said, "I'm sorry . . . did I understand you to say, sir, that the Soviets are not using Eastern Europe as their own sphere of influence in occupying most of the countries there?"

Ford responded: "I don't believe . . . that the Yugoslavians consider themselves dominated by the Soviet Union. I don't believe that the Romanians consider themselves dominated by the Soviet Union. I don't believe that the Poles consider themselves dominated by the Soviet Union. Each of these countries is independent, autonomous, it has its own territorial integrity, and the United States does not concede that those countries are under the domination of the Soviet Union."

Carter seized the opportunity, and he invited Ford to "convince the Polish Americans and the Czech Americans and the Hungarian Americans in this country that those countries don't live under the domination and supervision of the Soviet Union behind the Iron Curtain."

Ford also tried to deflect comments of his Eastern European/ Soviet Union misstatement. After his narrow defeat to

Carter, he was asked what he might do after the election, because there was talk that he might teach at the University of Michigan.

Ford said he had considered becoming a college professor but noted:

"I'm not going to teach Eastern European history, however."

LOCAL COLOR

"I might be paralyzed from the waist down, but unlike Gray Davis, I'm not paralyzed from the neck up."
—*Larry Flynt during his 2003 run for California governor*

Another Ford misstatement occurred when he addressed the National Athletic Association, an organization of athletic directors from the most prestigious colleges in America. Said Ford:

"I feel very much at home here today, because the athletic director of any college and the president of the United States have a great deal in common. We both need the talent, we both need the cooperation of others, and we both have a certain lack of performance in our jobs." (He should have said: "We both have a certain lack of 'permanence' in our jobs.")

Although Ford was an avid golfer, he tripped a lot on the links. He was able to make fun of himself, however:

"Arnold Palmer has asked me not to wear his slacks except under an assumed name. . . . They say you can tell a good golfer by the number of people in the gallery. You've heard of Arnie's Army. My group is called Ford's Few. . . . My problem is that I have a wild swing. Back home on my home course, they don't yell 'Fore,' they yell 'Ford!' . . . The Secret Service Men you see around me today—when I play golf, they qualify for combat pay. . . . In Washington I'm known as the President of the United States, and in golf I'm known as the Jinx of the Links."

Said Ford of Carter: "Teddy Roosevelt . . . once said, 'Speak softly and carry a big stick.' Jimmy Carter wants to speak loudly and carry a flyswatter."

Appearing before an audience during the Democratic presidential race, Carter said:

"I don't claim to be the man best qualified to be president of the United States. There are, right here in this room, people better qualified to be president than I am. And I want to thank you for not running this year: I've already got competition enough."

After voting in his home town of Plains, Georgia, reporters asked Carter for whom he voted. With a grin he said:

"I voted for Walter Mondale and his running mate."

After winning the Democratic presidential nomination, Carter returned home to find hundreds of reporters and others around his house. His daughter, Amy, set up a lemonade stand, and Carter said that she should double the price from five cents a glass to ten cents. When some reporters joked that they should get a discount, Carter said:

"Reporters should pay double, because they are on an expense account."

When he first ran for governor of Georgia, Jimmy Carter was largely unknown, and he observed:

"I was so unknown that some journalist labeled me 'Jimmy Who?'"

While campaigning in Mississippi during a very rushed time, Carter, seeking the Democratic nomination, shook the hand of a department-store mannequin. In the turmoil of the moment, he thought it was a voter. Once he realized his mistake, he said to his handlers:

"Better give her a brochure too."

While talking to reporters in Ohio on a press bus, Carter said:

"You've treated me very well so far."

"Compared to what?" one asked.

"To the way you treated Nixon."

Ruth Carter Stapleton, Carter's sister, complained about the rigorous campaign schedule, but so did her brother, who said:

"Honey, I can will myself to sleep until ten thirty a.m. and get my ass beat, or I can will myself to get up at six a.m. and become president."

In Atlanta he announced his candidacy before two thousand supporters, including astronaut Buzz Aldrin. Carter said:

"As of this time here, in the state that I love, surrounded by friends of mine from all over the nation—in fact, even from the moon—I want to announce that I am a candidate for the presidency of the United States."

Speaking before the United Rubber Workers Union, Carter was asked who his favorite vice president was. "Harry Truman," he said.

The crowd roared with laughter, and he apologized for making fun of the questions and said: "I know what you mean. But I think it would be presumptuous of me to start naming vice presidents when I haven't even got a nomination yet."

Carter aides tell this story of campaigning during the Iowa primary. Carter and two aides, Jody Powell and Greg Schneiders, arrived at an airstrip early one morning. Carter and Schneiders boarded the plane, and as it taxied down the runway, Schneiders said that Powell was not on board. Schneiders asked the pilot to radio the terminal and learned that Powell was inside, using the telephone. A few minutes later, Powell ran out of the terminal, caught up with the waiting plane, and climbed inside. Carter, who had been willing to take off without his press secretary, said:

"Jody, you've got one friend on this airplane—and it ain't me."

Speaking before an audience in New York, Carter said:

"If all the things the Republicans are saying about me are true, I wouldn't vote for me either."

LOCAL COLOR

"I could be an incredible voice in the Senate. Why? Because the media will cover me every single day."
—*Jerry Springer on his bid to become a senator from Ohio*

"I can promise you that when I go to Sacramento, I will *pump up* Sacramento!"
—*Arnold Schwarzenegger, during the California governor's race*

About campaigning, Carter noted:

"I have made my share of mistakes. If any of my supporters began this campaign believing I was infallible, I think I have by now disabused them of that notion. But that is as it should be. The American people should see the presidential candidate warts and all. We've had enough slickly packaged candidates. We should cast our vote for real people, not for images."

While campaigning for the Democratic nomination in Jackson, Mississippi, Carter appeared before a group of seventeen-year-olds and said:

"I grow peanuts over in Georgia. I'm the first child in my daddy's family who ever had a chance. I used to get up at four in the morning to pick peanuts. Then I'd walk three miles along the railroad track to deliver them. My house had no running water or electricity. . . . But I made it to the U.S. Naval Academy and became a nuclear physicist under Admiral Rickover. . . . Then I came back home to the farm and got interested in community affairs. . . .

"In 1970 I became Governor of Georgia with a campaign that appealed to all people. I reorganized the state government and proved that government could provide love and compassion to all people, black and white, because I believe in it. . . . Now I want to be your president. I hope you'll come see me. Please don't leave me up there in the White House all by myself."

Carter was being brutally honest when he said:
"Watch me closely during the campaign, because I won't be any better a president than I am a candidate."

Carter once noted:
"We were all fuzzy on the issues. That's proven by the fact that we [got] elected. The advantage of being a presidential candidate is that you have a much broader range of issues on which to be fuzzy."

Carter was very competitive and did not like losing:
"Show me a good loser, and I'll show you a loser."

This comes under the category of: Huh? Bob Dole debating Walter Mondale in October 1976:
"If we added up all the killed and wounded in Democrat

wars in this century, it would be about 1.6 million Americans, enough to fill the city of Detroit."

Carter took a lot of criticism for his brother Billy's heavy beer drinking and poor behavior. Speaking about his plans to reorganize the government, the candidate joked:

"I'd like to involve Billy in the government. I've been thinking of reorganizing and putting the CIA and the FBI together. But Billy said he wouldn't head up any agency he couldn't spell."

Carter acknowledged that Vice President Humphrey could be long-winded. He joked when he accepted the Democratic nomination:

"We must all pay tribute to Hubert Horatio Hornblower . . . uh, Humphrey."

Dole: "I used to call him [Carter] Southern-fried McGovern . . . but I have a lot of respect for Senator McGovern."

Comedians often mocked Carter's Southern accent, so he turned it around to his advantage—especially when campaigning in Southern states:

"Isn't it time," Carter asked, "that we had a president without an accent?"

Former Minnesota senator Eugene McCarthy once remarked, "It's dangerous for a national candidate to say things that people might remember."

After the New Hampshire primary, someone told Mc-Carthy that three dead men had voted in Manchester. "They were ours," said the Catholic senator. "It was a resurrection."

After the election, McCarthy wrote an article for the *New York Times* magazine titled "Ten Things a Candidate Should Know About New Hampshire":

1. New Hampshire is not a simple state. Like Gaul, it is divided into three parts: Massachusetts, Maine, and Vermont. In approaching New Hampshire for campaign purposes, a candidate must be aware that each of these states influences the economics of the towns directly across the border.

2. No matter when or how a candidate enters New Hampshire, he will either be met or soon found out by the *Manchester Union Leader* and its well-known publisher, William Loeb. [deceased]

3. Candidates should not enter New Hampshire too early. Visitors to the state in early fall are tolerated as leaf viewers.

4. Primary candidates should keep in mind that New Hampshire is a modest state, that it lives carefully, not trusting anyone with too much power. Although one of the smallest states in the Union, it has the largest legislative body. Candidates who promise too much are not likely to do well there.

5. New Hampshire is restrained in its claim to distinction. The *Information Please Almanac*, which all potential candidates for the New Hampshire primary should read, lists fruit and potatoes among its principal crops but makes no special claim as to quality or numbers.

6. Candidates must visit factories. In going through shoe and textile plants, they should be mindful of the observation of the poet Robert Lowell that, despite pay and working conditions, workers in shoe factories are happier than those working in textiles and clothing.

7. With energy a central issue, it will be especially important for candidates to be well informed about wood and wood-burning stoves.

8. New Hampshire is not for sale, nor does it seek approval . . .

9. Remember that a good winter driver experienced in ice and snow is much more important in New Hampshire than a good advance man or press secretary.

10. Finally, if, as a candidate, you think you feel a groundswell, be careful. It may be no more nor less than a frost heave.

Ronald Reagan said this about losing the 1976 Republican nomination to Ford:

"It's been said that if you put [President] Ford and me together in a dark room, you can't tell us apart philosophically. Well, if you turn on the lights, you can."

Bob Dole, the vice-presidential candidate said:

"When President Ford asked me to be his running mate, I asked my old friend Lyn Nofziger to join the Dole campaign team, and he readily agreed. 'We won't win,' he told a friend, 'but we'll have a lot of fun.'"

Acknowledging his loss in the presidential primaries, after finishing second in the fifth presidential primary in a row, Morris Udall said, "The voters have spoken—the bastards!"

Udall said of Carter's angelic demeanor:

"Carter was the first politician in memory to come complete with halo."

Udall was criticizing the way the Republican administration had run the economy when he said:

"What's the difference between a pigeon and an Iowa farmer? A pigeon can still make a deposit on a tractor."

Udall joked about this primary experience:

"Shortly after I announced my candidacy in New Hampshire, I walked into a local barbershop and began introducing myself:

"'Hi, I'm Mo Udall and I'm running for president.'

"'Yeah, we know,' says one of the hangers-on, 'we were laughing about that yesterday.'"

Udall summed up his chances this way:

"I'm a one-eyed Mormon Democrat from conservative Arizona, and you can't have a higher handicap than that."

LOCAL COLOR

"The bottom line is there have been a lot of nuts elected to the United States Senate."
—*Iowa Senator Charles Grassley, on why Republicans should not oppose Virginia GOP senate nominee Oliver North*

"I guess the truth can hurt you worse in an election than about anything that could happen to you."
—*Humorist Will Rogers*

Udall was asked about his "victory scenario," and he described it this way:

"I feel a little bit like the coach on the way to the stadium in a bus with his team. He doesn't know what sport they are going to play, who the opponent will be, or whether they will be playing on wood, ice, or grass. The rule books are still being mimeographed, and somebody asks him, 'What is your game plan?'"

On gun control, Udall opined:

"I find as I travel around the country that attitudes are changing. But I am, after all, the congressman from Tombstone, Arizona. . . . Maybe we ought to send Henry Kissinger to negotiate with the National Rifle Association."

On inflation controls, Udall said:

"The first thing we need to do is get a new administration in Washington and get to work on this problem. . . . Maybe we ought to turn inflation over to the Post Office. They may not stop it, but they'll damn well slow it down."

At a political breakfast in New Hampshire, Udall was asked by a cynical voter if he was a lawyer. Udall responded by telling the story about the politician who was campaigning and was told by a citizen that he would vote for him if he was "not one of those damn lawyers." The politician's response was, "Well, I'm a lawyer, but if it helps any, I'm not much of a lawyer."

Jimmy Carter's redneck brother, Billy, summed up his situation this way:

"I got a momma who joined the Peace Corps and went to India when she was sixty-eight. I got one sister [Ruth] who's a Holy Roller preacher. I got another sister [Gloria] who wears a helmet and rides a motorcycle. And I got a brother who thinks he's going to be president. So that makes me the only sane person in the family."

Johnny Carson noted that both Ford and Carter misspoke many times during the campaign. He said one night:

"I have a late score from the newsroom. Jimmy Carter is ahead of Gerald Ford, two blunders to one." Later, he remarked, "You know, the Carter–Ford election is going to be tough. It boils down to fear of the unknown versus fear of the known."

During Carter's inauguration a woman in the crowd was heard to say: "Isn't Rosalynn [Carter's wife] brave? She hasn't even got a hat on." Another person said: "Man, he got out and walked among the people like a man. Not like Nixon. He has got no reason to be scared."

Former president Johnson described Ford in this brutal way:

"So dumb, he can't fart and chew gum at the same time."

Eugene McCarthy noted:

"Being in politics is like being a football coach. You have to be smart enough to understand the game, and dumb enough to think it's important."

THE ELECTION OF 1980

RONALD REAGAN, Republican
43.9 million (489 electoral) George H. W. Bush

JIMMY CARTER, Democrat
36.5 million (49 electoral) Walter F. Mondale

JOHN B. ANDERSON, Independent
5.7 million (0 electoral) Patrick J. Lucey

After the malaise years of Carter, voters were looking for an upbeat candidate who didn't take things so darn seriously. They found hope in actor-turned-politician Ronald Reagan, a "Great Communicator" whose sense of humor gave Americans a reason to like politics again. Moreover, he made fun of his age, a self-effacing trait that really appealed to voters. During a televised Republican debate for the 1980 presidential nomination, Reagan remarked that wage and price controls had continually failed since the time of the Roman emperor Diocletian. And he added: "I'm the only one here old enough to remember."

Likewise, he repelled criticism that his age would make him forgetful after once telling supporters in Grand Rapids, Michigan, that he promised tax "increases" when he meant to say "decreases." He explained: "I've been talking about Carter so long that I make mistakes like he does."

Many voters did not like how Carter had been handling the economy; inflation and interest rates were both over 10 percent. Beltway insiders also took him to task as a micromanager who focused on small government issues while missing the point on larger ones. He was criticized for "giving away" the Panama Canal and signing what many considered unnecessary concessions to the Soviets in penning the SALT II Strategic Arms Limitation Treaty.

In foreign policy, Carter's biggest blunder may have been his reaction to the takeover in November 1979 of the U.S. embassy in Tehran by students who were angry about American support for the Shah of Iran. Many Americans saw Carter as a hypocrite touting human rights around the world while supporting the Shah, who ran a brutal regime.

Reagan promised to keep government out of the affairs of individual citizens and advocated lowering taxes. Because of his positive demeanor and clever wit, Reagan clicked with voters who wanted a change from Carter's hangdog attitude that was growing more sour by the day. Indeed, in July 1979, Carter—whose poll numbers were in the low 30s— delivered a national address that became known as the Malaise Speech. Although he never used that word, he gave a specially televised talk—the kind usually reserved for a crisis—and pronounced that "The solution of our energy crisis [gas lines were common, due to cutbacks by oil-producing nations] can also help us to conquer the crisis of the spirit in our country." He went on to say that the nation had a "crisis of confidence" and that Americans were too focused on materialism. Some people described it more as a sermon than a speech.

The immediate effect of the speech was positive, as it looked into the souls of Americans. Shortly thereafter, however, opinion-makers saw the speech as one coming from a loser. In contrast, Reagan applauded and exalted the American spirit in a way that got people excited, and he won the election. Anderson, running as an Independent, got a respectable 5.8 million votes but no electoral votes.

Pollsters also noted that the election was a turning point in American politics as they witnessed the rising power of the suburban voter as well as those in the Sun Belt. It also signaled a more solidified party posture with Democrats becoming more liberal and Republicans more conservative, with those on the fringes of their traditional parties jumping ship to the other.

Clearly, the turning point in the campaign was the second debate that had Carter on the defensive about the still-unresolved Iranian hostage crisis, nuclear arms treaties, and the economy. Carter told those in attendance how he consulted with his daughter, Amy, which then became the favorite subject of late-night comedians and political cartoonists. At almost every turn, Carter seemed downtrodden when compared with Reagan's sunny disposition.

What sealed the deal for Reagan was his final comment in the debate: "Are you better off now than you were four years ago?" This one single question resonated with voters, and pushed Reagan ahead in the polls and on to victory.

· · · · · · · · ·

Comedian Mort Sahl said of the election:

"Reagan won because he ran against Jimmy Carter. If he ran unopposed, he would have lost."

At a Gridiron Club banquet, Reagan told the crowd:

"I heard one presidential candidate say that what this

country needed was a president for the nineties. I was set to run again. I thought he said a president *in* his nineties."

Reagan spoke from experience when he said:
"Any candidate who says he isn't frightened is a liar or a fool."

Reagan used this line at several different occasions, depending upon who he was talking about:
"I haven't had Jimmy Carter's experience. I wouldn't be caught dead with it."

When President Carter and Ronald Reagan were both campaigning in Columbus, Ohio, on the same day, Reagan told his supporters:
"I heard some people are having trouble telling which motorcade is which. Well, his turns left at every corner."

Reagan was quick on the uptake with this quip in Chicago when his microphone broke:
"Why do I have the feeling that I'm fading out? [Vice President] Mondale isn't in the city by any chance, is he?"

Reagan shared this one with an enthusiastic crowd in Detroit:
"I had a dream the other night. I dreamed that Jimmy Carter came to me and asked why I wanted his job. I told him I didn't want his job. I wanted to be president."

In Middleburg, Virginia, Reagan jabbed Carter with this one:

"Carter was supposed to go on *60 Minutes* to talk about his accomplishments, but that left him with fifty-nine minutes to fill."

In Houston, Reagan gave this explanation of why Carter would not join the debate between him and John Anderson:

"President Carter has been debating candidate Carter for the past three and a half years—and losing."

After a prominent member of Carter's staff was accused of smoking marijuana, Reagan told a crowd in Topeka, Kansas:

"The president had ordered there be no hard liquor in the White House. And now we find some of the White House has been smoking pot. This is the first administration we can honestly say is high and dry."

Reagan told a campaign crowd that Carter had too many excuses for his failures while in office. Said Reagan: "It makes you wonder who's been in charge for the last three and a half years."

The audience shouted: "Amy! Amy!"—a reference to the president's remarks that his daughter had told him that nuclear proliferation was on her mind.

Reagan returned: "That could be. I know he touched our hearts, all of us, the other night. I remember when Patti and Ron were little tiny kids, we used to talk about nuclear power."

During a debate Reagan said:

"I know the president's supposed to be replying to me,

but sometimes I have a hard time in connecting what he's saying with what I have said my positions are. I sometimes think he's like the witch doctor that gets mad when a good doctor comes along with a cure that will work."

During one speech in New Jersey, Reagan directed his comments to Democrats:

"I know what it's like to pull the Republican lever for the first time, because I used to be a Democrat myself, and I can tell you it only hurts for a minute and then it feels just great."

Chiding Carter for his economic policies, Reagan noted:

"Depression is when you're out of work. A recession is when your neighbor's out of work. Recovery is when Carter's out of work."

LOCAL COLOR

"If I lose, I'm going to retire from politics, practice law, and wear bright leather pants."
—*Illinois senator Carol Moseley Braun*

"He did support me by endorsing my opponent."
—*Damon Baldone's response when asked if the governor of Louisiana, Mike Foster, endorsed him for the Louisiana legislature*

Reagan repeatedly took on the issue of his age with great aplomb:

"It was easier to run for president when I was a boy. Back then there were only thirteen states."

Said Reagan:

"I've never been able to understand why a Republican contributor is a 'fat cat,' and a Democratic contributor of the same amount of money is a 'public-spirited philanthropist.'"

Just before he assumed office, an adviser briefed Reagan on many problems facing the country. Reagan joked, "I think I'll demand a recount."

Reagan zinged Carter about the problem of unemployment in America:

"Carter said he'd do something about unemployment. He did. In April, 825,000 Americans lost their jobs."

During a debate in Cleveland, Reagan looked relaxed and full of confidence. When asked later if he was nervous about debating Carter he said:

"No, not at all. I've been on the same stage with John Wayne."

Heard during a debate:

WALTER MONDALE: George Bush doesn't have the manhood to apologize.

BUSH: Well, on the manhood thing, I'll put mine up against his any time.

Morris King "Mo" Udall was asked in 1980 if he would consider running again for president. He responded:

"If nominated, I will run to Mexico; if elected, I will fight extradition."

Reagan aide Michael Deaver tells the following story from his book *Behind the Scenes*:

"A little before nine on inauguration morning, Deaver arrived at Blair House to help the president-elect get ready for the inaugural ceremony. He found Mrs. Reagan getting her hair done and asked: 'Where's the governor?' Without looking around, Mrs. Reagan answered: 'I guess he's still in bed.' 'In bed?' exclaimed Deaver. 'If it was me, if I was about to become president of the United States, I don't think I could still be asleep at nine o'clock on the morning of my swearing in.'

"He opened the door to the pitch-dark bedroom, curtains drawn, with an indistinct heap of blankets on the bed. 'Governor?' he called. 'Yeah?' came the sleepy response. 'It's nine o'clock!' said Deaver. 'Yeah?' repeated Reagan. 'Well, you're going to be inaugurated in two hours.' Sighed Reagan: "'Does that mean I have to get up?'"

When asked his best qualification for being president, Reagan said:

"I'm not smart enough to lie."

George H. W. Bush dropped out of the presidential race when reports surfaced that a $300,000 accounting error left his campaign in debt. Bush said:

"There is something, though, that when you project income and it doesn't come in like you project, you have a revenue shortfall."

Comedian Bob Hope campaigned for Reagan and said:

"I don't know what people have against Jimmy Carter. He's done nothing."

After the campaign Bush described the experience this way:

"It's the feeling of being at the end of something."

Bush criticized Reagan for his economic plan that would lower taxes, increase military spending and balance the budget. This seemingly impossible situation was referred to by Bush as "voodoo economics." After he was chosen as Reagan's running mate he said of the phrase: "God, I wish I hadn't said that."

And he added: "It's the only memorable thing I've ever said, and I've regretted saying it."

Critical of the Democrats' handling of the economy, Reagan said:

"I was alarmed at my doctor's report. He said I was sound as a dollar."

During a primary debate in New Hampshire, Bush confused two very opposite words:

"We can now break the back of inflation, and we can increase employment. We are pessimistic."

During the primary, Bush alluded to his stint at the CIA and how it prepared him for being president:

"I'm going to be so much better a president for having been at the CIA that you're not going to believe it."

During the campaign, Bush told an audience at a South Carolina campus:

"I'll be glad to reply to or dodge your questions, depending on what I think will help our election most."

THE ELECTION OF 1984

RONALD REAGAN, Republican
43.9 million (525 electoral) George H. W. Bush

WALTER MONDALE, Democrat
37.6 million (13 electoral) Geraldine A. Ferraro

Having survived an assassination attempt just sixty-nine days into his presidency, and with the "Reagan Revolution" in full swing, Reagan was ready to take on the Democrats in the 1984 election. His wit was as sharp as ever, and he continued to deflect criticism of his age and, to some, his laissez-faire approach to governing. When Reagan's opponent, Walter Mondale, accused him of "government by amnesia," Reagan countered with: "I thought that remark accusing me of amnesia was uncalled for. I just wish I could remember who said it."

On another occasion Reagan quipped: "I will not make age an issue of this campaign. I am not going to exploit, for political purposes, my opponent's youth and inexperience."

However, the Reagan years were not good for everyone; 15.2 percent of the country lived in poverty—an increase of 13 percent since 1980—and tax cuts mainly favored the richest strata.

Still, Reagan was popular because of his genial nature and his hard line against Communism. Because people liked him, missteps and scandals were excused—including the disastrous decision to send troops to Lebanon and the ensuing death of 241 soldiers at a barracks—giving him the nickname

"Teflon President." As he did in 1980, Reagan chose George H. W. Bush for his vice president.

The Democratic field was crowded and included Jesse Jackson, Fritz Hollings, Gary Hart, Walter Mondale, George McGovern, and John Glenn. While Hart was a formidable foe, Mondale took him down a peg when he ran ads that piggybacked on a much-loved Wendy's ad campaign at the time, "Where's the beef?" in which Hart's programs and policies were labeled as being all fluff and little substance.

When Mondale finally got the nod, he chose Geraldine Ferraro as his vice-presidential running mate, the first woman from a major party to be so chosen.

Mondale's campaign was described as dreary and uninspiring. For the most part, he was the anti-Reagan, defining his policy as the opposite of what the incumbent believed but without the charisma to do it well. Many voters thought he was supporting the poor on the backs of the middle class, so he lost the votes of Southern Democrats and blue-collar workers in northern cities.

Many citizens believed that Mondale underestimated the Soviet threat and overemphasized the Equal Rights Amendment, which passed its deadline for approval in 1982. The fact that he had a woman as a running mate did not seem to add novelty—or woman voters—to his bid for the presidency.

Although Reagan was clearly representing the country's richer class with his economic plans, he appealed to all strata and tried to bolster his sway with working-class and younger people by using Bruce Springsteen's "Born in the USA" as a campaign song. Springsteen took issue and asked Reagan's campaign to stop.

The election's outcome was an embarrassment for Democrats. Mondale lost the electoral vote in every state except for Minnesota—his home state, which he won by fewer than 3,800 votes.

· · · · · · · · ·

After he lost the election, Mondale noted that television was a prime factor in his defeat:

"Modern politics today requires a mastery of television. I've never really warmed up to television. And in fairness to television, it's never warmed up to me."

Mondale offered a bleak critique of politics when he said:

"In our system, at about eleven thirty on election night, they just push you off the edge of the cliff—and that's it. You might scream on the way down, but you're going to hit the bottom, and you're not going to be in elected office."

Mondale lamented that once he was branded as a less-than-exciting candidate, there was not much he could do to change that image:

"Political image is like mixing cement. When it's wet, you can move it around and shape it, but at some point it hardens and there's almost nothing you can do to reshape it."

Mondale's campaign schedule was grueling, and he complained:

"I've traveled more this year than any other living human being, and if I'd traveled any more, I wouldn't be living."

Putting it another way, Mondale said:

"Running for president is physically, emotionally, mentally, and spiritually the most demanding single undertaking I can envisage, unless it's World War III."

Of his opponent, Mondale noted:

"You have got to be careful quoting Ronald Reagan, because when you quote him accurately it is called mudslinging."

Referring to the February 1984 Democratic presidential primary debate in New Hampshire, President Reagan told *Newsweek*: "There were so many candidates on the platform that there were not enough promises to go around."

Mondale and Ferraro were campaigning in Texas when they were joined by top Texas Democrats, including state treasurer Ann Richards and Lt. Governor Bill Hobby. Hobby joked: "If Reagan loved women any more, Ann Richards would have to take in ironing."

On taxes, Reagan quipped:

"Republicans believe every day is the Fourth of July, but Democrats believe every day is April 15."

When asked questions about her family's finances, Ferraro got into some trouble. Later she said:

"I should have had a circuitous answer that was a nonanswer."

Commenting on Reagan's economic theories sometimes referred to by detractors as "voodoo economics," Ferraro said:

"I'd call it a new version of voodoo economics, but I'm afraid that would give witch doctors a bad name."

After his debate with Ferraro, Bush said of the experience:

"Boy, I'm glad that thing is over! I don't need any more of that."

Comedian Robert Klein said of lackluster Mondale:

"I'm a little dubious about Walter Mondale. Even if he's elected, I'm not sure Ms. Ferraro will find enough for him to do."

LOCAL COLOR

"To be perfectly blunt, I'm much more intelligent."
—*Dawn Clark Netsch, 1994 Democratic candidate for governor of Illinois, explaining why she was better qualified for the job than incumbent Jim Edgar. Edgar was reelected.*

Comedian Robin Williams said of Ferraro, who was enduring a lot of sexist remarks and jokes:

"We'd never go to war, and every twenty-eight days we'd have severe negotiations."

Comedian David Steinberg put in his two cents with this one:

"Walter Mondale is getting increasingly desperate. He knows he's in trouble. He just announced that if elected he will marry Geraldine Ferraro. Or, if the people of San Francisco prefer, Gary Hart."

Satirist songwriter Mark Russell noted:

"Mr. Mondale has said that God doesn't belong in politics, and apparently God feels the same way about Mr. Mondale."

Russell added this about the beginning days of the campaign:

"Mondale started slowly . . . then he tapered off."

THE ELECTION OF 1988

GEORGE H. W. BUSH, Republican
48.9 million (426 electoral) J. Danforth Quayle

MICHAEL S. DUKAKIS, Democrat
41.9 million (111 electoral) Lloyd Bentsen

I f we needed to be reminded of two campaign truths—
that the public's first impressions of a candidate are diffi-
cult to change and negative advertising works—the 1988
election brought it home once again.

The Republican Bush wasted no time in portraying
Democrat Dukakis as a "liberal" who was soft on defense.
Dukakis, in response, tried to show the public that being a
liberal meant being strong on defense, and he did so by riding
in a tank. But with his helmeted head popping out of the tank
hatch like a bobblehead doll and waving to the crowd, he
looked downright silly, out of place, and ineffectual as a potential commander in chief. In fact, the footage was so weak
that the Bush campaign used it in their ads, with voiceovers
that ridiculed the Massachusetts governor's ability to lead.

The Republicans were not without their own mistakes;
the selection of J. Danforth Quayle as vice president, for instance. Dan Quayle put his foot in his mouth on a regular
basis, looking so much like a buffoon, that the Democrats
used footage of the young senator with the tag line: "Quayle:
just a heartbeat away."

Dukakis's choice for vice president was Texas senator
Lloyd Bentsen. Bentsen was chosen over the objection of
Jesse Jackson, who had come in second in the nomination

voting. Dukakis picked him reportedly to help bring in Texas's large electoral bloc. (It didn't work.)

As the campaign progressed, Dukakis suffered many setbacks, including a bout of flu before the second debate that made him look lethargic and dispassionate; the resignation of staffer Donna Brazile after she spread rumors that Bush had had an extramarital affair; and, most important, criticism leveled against Dukakis for support of a prison furlough program that he had instituted while governor. The program allowed the release of Willie Horton, a convicted murderer who, while on furlough, committed rape and assault in Maryland. Republican ads played up the Willie Horton issue, showing that Dukakis was "too liberal" on crime and exhibited poor judgment on social issues.

Many observers suggest that Bush did not win the election as much as Dukakis lost it. Bush was riding a wave of relative peace and economic prosperity brought on by a very popular Ronald Reagan, and Dukakis kept shooting himself in the foot.

Final result: Bush and Quayle won by a substantial majority.

• • • • • • • • •

Bush's astute observation of the election:

"It's no exaggeration to say the undecideds could go one way or another."

Two months before the election, Quayle told a Springfield, Illinois, audience:

"Republicans understand the importance of the bondage between parent and child."

One of the most exciting moments in the campaign was during the vice-presidential debate. Quayle tried to deflect criticism that he was too inexperienced to be vice president, and he likened himself to John F. Kennedy—who had served fourteen years in Congress, compared to Quayle's twelve years.

"I have as much experience in the Congress as Jack Kennedy did when he sought the presidency," Quayle said.

Bentsen responded, "Senator, I served with Jack Kennedy. I knew Jack Kennedy. Jack Kennedy was a friend of mine. Senator, you're no Jack Kennedy."

The crowd roared at Bentsen's perfect delivery.

Quayle then said, "That was really uncalled for, Senator."

To which Bentsen responded, "You are the one that was making the comparison, Senator, and I'm the one who knew him well. And frankly I think you are so far apart in the objectives you choose for your country that I did not think the comparison was well-taken."

Comedian Mark Russell added onto the Bentsen assessment of Quayle: "Hell, he's no *Caroline* Kennedy."

Dukakis had a sense of humor about his appearance:

"I had to run for president to find out my eyebrows had become a status symbol." He smiled. "If you can't remember my name, and can't pronounce it, just remember: Go for the guy with the bushy eyebrows."

Dukakis's one-liner about Bush:

"If he keeps this up, he's going to be the Joe Isuzu of American politics." (Joe Isuzu was a popular character in TV spots who told outrageous lies right to your face—with a smile.)

Congressman Eugene McCarthy offered this pessimistic view of the election:

"If the voter is in despair, or near it, he or she might follow the advice of the man in the gold breastplate under the old stone cross, as reported by William Butler Yeats: 'Stay at home and drink your beer and let the neighbors vote.'"

Describing how he handled his loss in the New Hampshire primary, Bob Dole said:

"I slept like a baby: Every two hours I woke up and cried."

Jack Kemp said of Bob Dole:

"In a recent fire, Bob Dole's library burned down. Both books were lost. And he hadn't even finished coloring one of them yet."

The award for stating the obvious goes to Quayle, who said:

"A low voter turnout is an indication of fewer people going to the polls."

Eugene McCarthy was being satirical and bitter when he wrote this article about the 1988 election, titled "Who Won the Election?"

"Those who may try to determine the political significance of the 1988 election may be looking at an aspect, perhaps as I did in 1982, of secondary importance. The truly important struggle may be, as it was in 1982, among the three major television networks. The competition involved areas of measurable superiority or failure: (1) Nielsen ratings; (2) earliest predictions of the outcome of the election, either in individual contests or in overall gains and losses of the two parties; and (3) best scores of right over wrong predictions, with some adjustment and a greater margin of error allowed to networks making early mistakes than was allowed to those who persisted in error, or made late mistakes."

At a campaign stop, Dole heard the theme from *Star Wars* and said:

"Hey, we got vision! We even got vision music!"

A few days before the campaign's end, Bush said to reporters in a semi-farewell speech:

"It's been such a long journey, so many twenty-four-hour days, and there are so many times I'd see you scrambling for a bus in the darkness or shivering in your parkas on a tarmac somewhere at dawn, and I'd think: That's tough. Too bad. It's not my problem. Get a job. Get a haircut."

LOCAL COLOR

"A chess tournament disguised as a circus."
—*British journalist Alistair Cooke's description of a political convention*

"Vote: the instrument and symbol of a freeman's power to make a fool of himself and a wreck of his country."
—*Ambrose Bierce, American satirist*

At the GOP convention, Bush made his famous "No New Taxes" pledge. ("Read My Lips . . .") Two years later as president he reversed course, accepting a tax increase to reduce the deficit. One day while jogging, a reporter asked him about it and turned the question back when he pointed to his backside and said: "Read my hips."

A few minutes into the first debate, Bush said to Dukakis: "Is this the time to unleash our one-liners?"

He then decided to bash Dukakis for the poor environmental conditions in his native Boston by saying: "That answer was about as clear as Boston Harbor."

During the campaign, Bush joked about his blue-blood lineage. He said that his forebears landed at Ellis Island on the *Mayflower* when it made a quick stop before landing at Plymouth Rock. "My people were the ones waving the Bloomingdale's shopping bags."

Dole ridiculed Bush for saying he was from Texas when he was actually born in Massachusetts and raised in Connecticut. Dole stated:

"Of course, you could say *I* was from Texas. I was stationed at Camp Barkley, near Abilene, in the war. I got to Texas before George Bush."

Quayle was trying to say something clever, but it turned out wrong when he said of the ticket:

"In George Bush you get experience, and with me you get—The Future!"

Noted Quayle:

"One word sums up probably the responsibility of any vice president, and that one word is 'to be prepared.'"

Quayle told this joke about running for his first congressional seat in 1976. Talking to a voter in New Haven, Indiana, the candidate stuck out his hand and said:

"I'm Dan Quayle from Huntington. I'm running for Congress, and I'd like you to vote for me."

The man said: "Well, I was going to vote for you until I found out that you were a lawyer."

To which Quayle responded: "I am a lawyer, but I don't practice law."

The voter, who had until now feigned interest, was truly interested: "Well, what do you do?" he asked.

"I publish a newspaper," said Quayle.

"That's worse," said the voter.

Another Quayle gaffe:

"In a weird way, Ozzy [Osbourne] is a great anti-drug promotion. Look at him and how fried his brains are from taking drugs all those years and everyone will say, 'I don't want to be like that.'"

Said Mario Cuomo, then governor of New York:

"Pat Robertson calls for a moral reawakening. He sees debauchery, pornography, and prostitution. And things are even worse *outside* the evangelical movement." Robertson had claimed the ability to speak "in tongues," and Cuomo observed, "If he became president, we would finally have someone who could communicate with William F. Buckley."

LOCAL COLOR

"Constantly choosing the lesser of two evils is still choosing evil."

—*Musician Jerry Garcia*

"I never vote for anybody—I always vote against."

—*Actor W. C. Fields*

Jesse Jackson characterized conservatives this way:

"If this were Germany, we would call it fascism. If this were South Africa, we would call it racism. Here we call it conservatism."

When asked if he had something nice to say about his opponent during the debate, Bush said this about Dukakis:

"The concept of the Dukakis family has my great respect."

Bentsen explained why Republicans fear debates with Democrats:

"Why do Republicans fear debate? For the same reason baloney fears the slicer."

Bruce Babbitt, then governor of Arizona, said of the primary debates:

"Our debates have been like the mating of pandas in the zoo—the expectations are high, there's a lot of fuss and commotion, but there's never any kind of result."

At a fund-raising event, Jesse Jackson asked for donations in this way:

"A check or credit card, a Gucci bag strap, anything of value will do. Give as you live."

Bill Clinton, in a speech that many thought was too long, in which he nominated Dukakis at the convention:

"It wasn't my finest hour. It wasn't even my finest half hour."

Bush adviser Rich Bond on Dukakis's lack of experience in foreign policy:

"Michael Dukakis thinks a foreign market is a place to go for French bread."

Columnist Art Buchwald cited a letter he had received from one of his readers that asked: "What will happen to Murphy Brown once the election is over?"

Noted Buchwald: "The inside dope is that if there is a Bush–Quayle victory, Murphy will join the U.S. Navy Tailhook Association in hopes of finding a suitable father for her child."

In an attempt to curry the vote of Christian fundamentalists, Bush said of Jerry Falwell:

"The nation is in crying need of your moral vision!"

Richard Gephardt made fun of Dukakis's diminutive stature by saying:

"He can stand eye-to-eye—with my daughter."

Johnny Carson noted that the campaign was becoming dirtier as the days passed. He joked: "Bush is trying to paint Dukakis as unpatriotic. Today he accused Dukakis of mooning Mom's Apple Pie."

Republican media adviser Roger Ailes on the Democratic nominees:

"If those guys were on *The Dating Game*, nobody would get picked."

A Bush mix-up:

"When I'm the education president, you'll be able to send your college to children."

Here's another one. Bush got his months mixed up when on September 7, 1988, he referred to the Japanese attack on Pearl Harbor forty-seven years earlier. The attack was on December 7, 1941.

"Today, you remember—I wonder how many remember—today is Pearl Harbor Day—forty-seven years ago from this very day we were hit and hit hard at Pearl Harbor. And we were not ready."

During a debate with Dukakis, Bush made fun of his Pearl Harbor misspeak:

"We are going to make some changes and some tough choices before we go to deployment on the Midgetman missile—or on the Minuteman, whatever it is. We're going to have to—the MX—we're going to have to do that. It's Christmas. Wouldn't it be nice to be perfect? Wouldn't it be nice to be the Iceman [Dukakis] so you never make mistakes? These are the— These are the— These are the— My answer is do not make these unilateral cuts."

Comedian Alan King chimed in with:

"There is only one problem with this year's presidential election—one of the candidates has to win."

LOCAL COLOR

"Nothing is so abject and so pathetic as a politician who has lost his job, save only a retired stud horse."
—*Humorist H. L. Mencken*

"A straw poll only shows which way the hot air blows."
—*Author O. Henry*

On people's suggestions that he become more lively, Bush said:

"To kind of suddenly try to get my hair colored, and dance up and down in a miniskirt or do something—you know, show that I've got a lot of jazz out there and drop a bunch of one-liners . . . I'm running for the president of the United States. I kind of think I'm a scintillating kind of fellow." He went on to say: "What's wrong with being a boring kind of guy?"

And again, recognizing his lack of energy, Bush noted at a Los Angeles campaign rally:

"We're delighted to be here, Barbara and I. There's a danger: You have President Reagan, Governor Deukmejian, and George Bush. Watch out—overdose of charisma! That's not too good."

During his debate with Dukakis, Bush meant to say that three people in the race understood defense issues: himself,

Bentsen, and Quayle—an obvious dig at Dukakis. But it came out like this:

"There are three people on our ticket that are knowledgeable in the race, knowledgeable in defense, and Dan Quayle is one of them."

It's not clear what Bush meant when he said this during a debate with Dukakis:

"Those are two hyporhetorical questions."

From Bush's acceptance speech at the GOP convention in New Orleans comes the following. He was well aware of his less-than-dynamic demeanor:

"I'll try to hold my charisma in check."

At a campaign rally in Texas, Bush said:

"In New Hampshire I said I am one of you. I grew up in that part of the country. So I was armed tonight. But they wouldn't let me use credentials—my Texas hunting license, my Texas driver's license, and my voter's registration card."

Bush was asked if he would relax environmental rules if he became president. He said:

"Not with the idea of going back and killing off the fish or something, but seeing if we can't find the balance."

Asked several years before the election why he would make a good president, George H. W. Bush said:

"Well, I've got a big family, and lots of friends."

When another person asked why he would make a good president, Bush responded:

"If Carter can do it with no credentials, I can do it with these fantastic credentials. The fact that nobody else knows it is kind of discouraging."

When someone in the crowd screamed at Al Gore, then a senator from Tennessee, that he would make the perfect vice president instead of president, he responded:

"That was the ultimate heckle."

About his opponent, Bush said, "Michael Dukakis speaks Spanish. I wish I did. But I have three grandchildren, my blood coursing through their veins, who are half Mexican."

Michael Lawrence, one of Quayle's professors at DePauw University, said this about his former student, now selected to run for vice president:

"As vapid a student as I can recall."

In response to reporters asking about the Holocaust, Quayle said:

"The Holocaust was an obscene period in our nation's history. I mean this century's history. But we all lived in this century. I didn't live in this century."

Quayle told reporters that he would have to be more careful in his choice of words:

"Verbosity leads to unclear, matriculate things."

At a speech in Chicago, Quayle explained his views on deterring nuclear war:

"Right now we have a theory of mutually assured destruction that supposedly provides for peace and stability, and it's worked. But that doesn't mean that we can't build upon a concept of MAD where both sides are vulnerable to another attack. Why wouldn't an enhanced deterrent, a more stable peace, a better prospect to denying the ones who enter conflict in the first place to have a reduction of offensive systems and an introduction to defensive capability. I believe that is the route this country eventually will go."

Just after the election, Vice President Quayle said:

"One learns every day. Experience is a great teacher. By experience you learn. But as I enter office, I'm prepared now. Obviously, I will be more prepared as time goes on. I will know more about the office of the presidency. But I'm prepared now, and I will be more prepared as time goes on."

Mario Cuomo said of Bush before he won the election: "The vice president is sensitive to the needs of the poor. He has promised a new program to deal with the economic hardships of America's poor. The slogan is 'Just Say No to Poverty.'"

Mark Russell said of Quayle: "The media is backing off Dan Quayle. They're afraid of another backlash. So they're only asking him questions they think he can handle. Like, How many teams are in the Big 10?"

THE ELECTION OF 1992

WILLIAM J. CLINTON, Democrat
44.9 million (370 electoral) Albert A. Gore Jr.

GEORGE H. W. BUSH, Republican
39.2 million (168 electoral) J. Danforth Quayle

H. ROSS PEROT, Independent
19.7 million (0 electoral) James B. Stockdale

The election of 1992 will be remembered for the independent candidacy of eccentric Texas businessman H. Ross Perot, who waged an on-again, off-again campaign and brought color to an already lively election season. Perot was the master of jokes and one-liners, some intentional and some not, that were very typical of his brash, fresh way of looking at politics. He even made fun of his own appearance, including his small stature and large ears. In the first debate, Perot stated, "I don't have any experience in running up a four-trillion-dollar debt." The crowd laughed, and when he was asked about his proposal to pay off the deficit with an increased gasoline tax he said, "If there's a fairer way, I'm all ears."

We also saw word gaffes that were the hallmark of Bush's presentations. For example, on the environment Bush said, "That's why I'll be a great conservative and environmental president. I plan to fish and hunt as much as I can."

Bush had angered many of his conservative backers by breaking his 1988 campaign promise: "Read my lips. No new taxes," so he moved even further to the right in an attempt to recover. To that end, he allowed conservative journalist Pat Buchanan to give the opening speech at the convention in which he espoused his belief that the Bill and Hillary Clinton team would build an America that would encourage and embrace "radical feminism" and "environmental extremists." This so-called culture-war speech pushed many moderate Republicans to vote for Clinton.

Pushing aside an early bid for the nomination by Buchanan and white supremacist and Louisiana House of Representatives member David Duke, Bush again chose to run with Vice President Dan Quayle.

Arkansas governor Bill Clinton chose Tennessee senator Albert A. Gore as his running mate after repelling bids from California governor Jerry Brown and Massachusetts senator Paul Tsongas.

Clinton ran his campaign as a centrist, hoping to appeal to Democrats as well as moderate Republicans who rejected their party's move to the right. Although Bush's incursion into Iraq, the First Gulf War, was successful in the eyes of many, it did little to propel his candidacy.

But Clinton's main message to his campaigners was "It's the economy, stupid"—a mantra that spurred them to hammer away at Bush's inability to stem a recession and his refusal to consider greater federal involvement in health care. Quite simply, Clinton was selling change.

When billionaire Perot entered the fray, he used his own money to advertise and appeared on such popular shows as CNN's *Larry King Live* to sell his candidacy. He was fond of exhibiting charts and graphs showing how he would run the country. To many people he was a bit loopy, but to others, he was a refreshing change from professional, polished politicians. Early polls had Perot in the lead, something no third-party candidate had ever accomplished in nearly a century, but he hurt his chances when he announced he would not run—and then he changed his mind and reentered the race. Many of his most passionate supporters left and never returned, after suspecting that this unconventional candidate might quit again without warning.

Perot made history, though. Not only was he the first independent candidate to appear on a televised debate with the major candidates (John Anderson debated Ronald Reagan in 1980 when Jimmy Carter refused to engage in a three-man debate—one reason Carter lost the election to Reagan), but he also received about 20 percent of the popular vote. This feat was surpassed only by Theodore Roosevelt, who ran as a Progressive in the 1912 election and received almost half of the popular vote. (Democrat Woodrow Wilson won that race.)

Clinton's win ended twelve years of Republican control of the presidency. With his election, the Democrats also took control of Congress.

· · · · · · · · · ·

When it was said during the campaign that Vice President Quayle intended to be "a pit bull" against opponents, Clinton joked, "That's got every fire hydrant in America worried."

Clinton was smart enough to be self-deprecating about his intelligence. At one event, after being introduced as the smartest of the Democratic presidential candidates, he said, "Isn't that like calling Moe the most intelligent of the Three Stooges?"

At his Republican National Convention speech, Reagan joked:

"Tonight is a very special night for me. Of course, at my age, every night's a very special night."

Commenting on the Democratic ticket, George H. W. Bush stated:

"My dog Millie knows more about foreign affairs than these two bozos."

Referring to Clinton's famous remark that he smoked marijuana but did not inhale, Ronald Reagan told the Republican National Convention:

"When you see all that rhetorical smoke billowing up from the Democrats, well, ladies and gentlemen, I'd follow the example of their nominee: Don't inhale."

In his speech at the Republican National Convention, Newt Gingrich stated:

"If Thomas Edison had invented the electric light in the age of the welfare state, the Democrats would immediately introduce a bill to protect the candlemaking industry. The Democratic ticket would propose a tax on electricity—in fact, Al Gore does propose a tax on electricity. Ralph Nader would warn that electricity can kill; and at least one news report would begin, "'The candlemaking industry was threatened today.'"

Gingrich attacked the Democratic candidates this way:

"Wow, there are two salient facts about our next choice. . . . Fact number one is for four years he's [President

Bush has] gone to a pharmacy controlled by Democrats, and the Democrats have given him no medicine or they've given him bad medicine. Fact number two, the alternative doctors in town, Dr. Feelgood and Dr. Smilegood, are nice young guys, [they] have a terrific, guaranteed quick diet plan— twenty-eight-pound weight loss. The problem is, when you read the fine print, they get to the weight loss by amputating your leg. And the question is: Am I really eager enough to have a chance that I'll risk having my leg amputated?"

Reagan added, cleverly referring to an infamous quip from the 1984 debates:

"This fellow [Clinton] they've nominated claims he's the new Thomas Jefferson. Well, let me tell you something; I knew Thomas Jefferson. He was a friend of mine, and Governor, you're no Thomas Jefferson!"

LOCAL COLOR

"Asking an incumbent member of Congress to vote for term limits is a bit like asking a chicken to vote for Colonel Sanders."
—*South Carolina representative Bob Inglis*

"A man walked up to me on a Memphis street, slapped me on the back, pumped my hand vigorously and said: "'If I'd know'd you was going to win, I'd of voted for you.'"
—*Representative Dan Kuykendal of Tennessee*

Bush said, "[Clinton] says he wants to tax the rich, but folks, he defines 'rich' as anyone who has a job. You've heard of the separation of powers. My opponent practices a different theory: 'The power of separations.' Government has the power to separate you from your wallet."

At one point in the campaign, Quayle had gone on the offensive against the fictional main character in the TV sitcom *Murphy Brown* (played by Candace Bergen) because she was an unwed mother. The ensuing feud between the show's star and Quayle continued for some time. When Bush–Quayle's chances were looking dim, the vice president joked: "Actually, I'm envious of Murphy Brown. At least she's guaranteed of coming back this fall."

When asked what he would do about the country's deficit, Perot said this at the University of Richmond in Virginia:

"Well, we're $4 trillion in debt. We're going into debt an additional $1 billion—a little more than a billion dollars every working day of the year. . . .

"Now, it's not the Republicans' fault, of course. And it's not the Democrats' fault. And what I'm looking for is, who did it? Now, they're the two folks involved, so maybe if you put them together, they did it.

"Now, the facts are, we have to fix it. I'm here tonight for these young people up there in the balcony from this college. When I was a young man, when I got out of the Navy, I had multiple job offers. Young people [today] with high grades can't get a job.

"Now, whose fault is that? Not the Democrats', not the

Republicans'. Somewhere out there there's an extraterrestrial that's doing this to us, I guess. And everybody says they take responsibility. Somebody, somewhere has to take responsibility for this. [I'll] put it to you bluntly, American people. If you want me to be your president, we're going to face some problems, we'll deal with the problems, we'll solve our problems. We'll pay down our debt. We'll pass on the American dream to our children, and I will not leave our children a situation that they have today.

"When I was a boy, it took two generations to double the standard of living. Today, it will take twelve generations. Our children will not see the American dream because of this debt that somebody, somewhere dropped on us."

At a fund-raising event, Bush made the following statement as a lead-in to his talk on "family values":

"Somebody—somebody asked me . . . What's it take to win? I said to them, 'I can't remember, what does it take to win the Super Bowl?' Or maybe Steinbrenner, my friend George, will tell us what it takes for the Yanks to win—one run. But I went over to the strawberry festival this morning and ate a piece of shortcake over there—able to enjoy it right away. And once I completed it, it didn't have to be approved by Congress—I just went ahead and ate it—and that leads me into what I want to talk to you about today . . ."

Buchanan said of Bush, his rival for the Republican nomination:

"Left unscripted, Bush comes off as phony as a novice urban cowboy at Gilley's."

Buchanan and Quayle mixed it up when the vice president called Buchanan Pat the Hun for his far-right opinions. Buchanan responded by saying that he did not want to engage in a war of words.

Buchanan said: "I don't want to say anything critical of Dan Quayle. I don't want to be charged with child abuse."

Trump on Perot:

"I think he's going to have a helluva chance of getting elected, because frankly, I'm not sure that there is an alternative."

On a famous visit to a New Jersey classroom, Quayle misspelled "potato" by placing an "e" on the end and correcting a student who had spelled it correctly. Senator Tom Harken joked that Dan Quayle should sing the old song "Old McDonald Had a Farm" as "e-i-e-i-o . . . e." The TV show *Murphy Brown* ended its season premiere with a thousand pounds of potatoes unloaded on Quayle's doorstep. The joke continued with Clinton's acceptance speech, where he was talking about the advantage his ticket had over Bush's. Said Clinton: "He doesn't have Al Gore, but I do. Just in case you didn't notice, that's 'Gore' with an 'e' at the end."

While campaigning for reelection, Bush tried not to mention Clinton by name, so he tried to describe him geographically. However, there is no state between Oklahoma and Texas:

"I've referred occasionally to my opponent as 'the other guy' and even 'the governor of a certain state with a profitable chicken industry on the Mississippi River located somewhere between Texas and Oklahoma.'"

Bush meant to say "reception" during a campaign stop in Ridgewood, New Jersey:

"I don't want to run the risk of ruining what is a lovely recession."

Clinton was known for giving long speeches, and he accepted that criticism with this comment at Bush's expense:

"Mr. Bush says the election should be about trust, and I believe that's right. But for George Bush to say the election should be about trust is like me saying it should be about short speeches."

Perot had blurted out that if he were elected, there would be no gays in the cabinet or in the upper echelons of his administration. He noted that he had admonished his own company's executives that adulterers would be weeded out. Perot said: "How can I trust you if your wife can't trust you?"

The *National Review* said of Perot's pronouncements: "Ross Perot won't hire gays and adulterers for his administration. At last—a practical plan to shrink the size of government."

LOCAL COLOR

"Now, a delegate is bad enough, but an alternate is just a spare tire for a delegate. An alternate is the lowest form of political life there is. He is the parachute on a plane that never leaves the ground."
—*Humorist Will Rogers*

"Between Tom Campbell and Sonny Bono, they have the bad-haircut vote sewn up."
—*Joe Gelman, adviser to California Republican state senate candidate Bruce Herschensohn during the Republican primary in 1991*

To a group of scientists at Sandia National Labs, Bush said:

"I'm just waiting for one of you to come up with a robot that can give a public speech. I'm sure it will make my life easier and also yours."

Letting voters know where he stood, Buchanan stated:

"I am in Washington, not of it. No insider challenges an incumbent president. That makes me, de facto, an outsider."

On the chances of resuming his presidential run [which he did], Perot said:

"This is like saying how likely am I to jump over a tall building in a single bound—unlikely. This is like asking, Is lightning going to strike here in the next two seconds—I don't think so."

Said Clinton of having a new president in office:

"After the election . . . there'll be nobody to make fun [of]."

The *Pittsburgh Press* ran a cartoon showing an unkempt, beer-bellied voter in a recliner, complaining: "I'm sick and tired of politicians who are out of touch with the common man. I'm voting for that Texas billionaire."

Perot was a favorite of late-night comedians, including Jay Leno, who made light of his on-again, off-again campaign. Leno joked: "Ross Perot said the country would be better off if more politicians were like him. I couldn't agree more. I wish they'd all quit." He added: "A recent survey shows that Ross Perot is still the favorite among young single males. Sure, they can't make a commitment either."

Again harping on Perot's departure and reentry into the race, Leno joked about how Perot decided to allow his supporters to choose a campaign symbol. Said Leno: "How about the Yugo? The Yugo is small, it's funny-looking, and you never know when it's going to quit on you."

Leno added: "A lot of Ross Perot's volunteers are unhappy. They just figured out they're doing volunteer work for a billionaire."

Vice President Quayle was disputing candidate Clinton's suggestion that the nation should look to Hawaii's system as a model for health-care reform:

"Hawaii is a unique state. It is a small state. It is a state that is by itself. It is a—it is different than the other states. Well, all states are different, but it's got a particularly unique situation."

Buchanan's suggestion for immigration reform:

"I will stop this massive illegal immigration cold. Period. Paragraph. I'll build that security fence, and we'll close it and we'll say, 'Listen José, you're not coming in!' "

Buchanan at his sarcastic best:

"In this campaign, I have been called an anti-Semite, a homophobe, a racist, a sexist, a nativist, a protectionist, an isolationist, a social fascist, and a beer-hall conservative. And then Sam Donaldson had the nerve to ask me on the Brinkley show if I was insensitive, too."

And more about Perot from Leno: "Are you excited about Perot getting back in the race? That has all the excitement of finding out that Ford is going to start making Pintos again."

In a fund-raising letter Pat Robertson wrote:

"The feminist agenda is not about equal rights for women. It is about a socialist, anti-family political movement that encourages women to leave their husbands, kill their children, practice witchcraft, destroy capitalism, and become lesbians."

Leno also mocked Bush's economic plans. He told how he had received a chain letter: "It says put $500 in an envelope and send it to the name on the top of the list. And then I realized this wasn't a chain letter. This is President Bush's new economic plan."

Said comedian Mark Russell of the eccentric Perot: "All the candidates have military endorsements. Admiral Crowe supports Clinton; General Schwarzkopf is backing Bush. Cap'n Crunch is for Perot."

At a Bush–Quayle fund-raiser, Bush defended his idea to offer oil companies access to the Alaskan Wildlife Preserve for drilling, despite opposition from environmental groups. He told the audience:

"If you're worried about caribou, take a look at the arguments that were used about the pipeline. They'd say the caribou would be extinct. You've got to shake them away with a stick. They're all making love, lying up against the pipeline and you got thousands of caribou up there."

The press was reporting that Perot used private investigators to dig up dirt on competitors and even his own children. This prompted comedian Mark Russell to mention a newspaper headline he read that said:

"PEROT BAILOUT BOOSTS UNEMPLOYMENT.

FIFTY PRIVATE DETECTIVES LAID OFF."

Mark Russell again: "Everyone wondered how Ross Perot's followers could have allowed themselves to be conned by him. Perhaps it was because Jim and Tammy Bakker are out of business."

LOCAL COLOR

"Voting is simply a way of determining which side is stronger without putting it to the test of fighting."
—*Satirist H. L. Mencken*

"Public-opinion pollsters are people who count the grains of sand in your bird cage and then try to tell you how much sand there is on the beach."
—*Comedian Fred Allen*

Riffing on Perot's somewhat paranoid personality and penchant for secrecy, Mark Russell joked:

"He had learned that Martians were planning to jump out of his daughter's wedding cake.... Further dirty tricks included the distribution of a doctored photograph showing the head of Ross Perot attached to the body of a rational person."

Satirist Dave Barry said of Bush's ill-fated campaign:

"I can't blame the president for being a little bitter. It had to be hard being rejected after running such a strong campaign, such a shrewdly organized campaign, with his keen tacticians, Wayne and Garth."

While campaigning in New Hampshire during the primary, Bush talked about the importance of prayer:

"You cannot be president of the United States if you don't have faith. Remember Lincoln, going to his knees in times of trial and the Civil War and all that stuff. You can't be. And we are blessed. So don't feel sorry for—don't cry for me, Argentina."

Many Republicans were alarmed at how far right their party had drifted, citing the speech by Pat Buchanan who spoke of a cultural holy war. Writer Dave Barry opined:

"The perception on the part of the public was that the convention had been dominated a little too much by the religious right, especially as they opened the second night by burning a suspected witch."

Said Jay Leno of Perot's campaign strategy:

"The rumor is, to boost his approval rating, he may announce he's a lesbian."

Admiral Stockdale, like Perot, emphasized their "outsider" status to voters as shown during the vice president's debate. ABC's Hal Bruno was the moderator:

HAL BRUNO: Admiral Stockdale, your opening statement, please, sir?

ADMIRAL STOCKDALE: Who am I? Why am I here? [Laughter and applause] I'm not a politician—everybody knows that. So don't expect me to use the language of the Washington insider. Thirty-seven years in the Navy, and only one of them up there in Washington. And now I'm an academic.

During a fund-raiser in Houston, Bush discussed the Republican versus Democratic view of unemployment legislation:

"The Democrats want to ram it down my ear in a political victory."

Iowa senator Tom Harkin dropped his bid because of insufficient funds and said:

"When you're out of Bud, you're out of beer."

After the election, the Clintons joined the Gores in Charlottesville, Virginia, for their inauguration bus caravan to Washington, D.C., which would end at the Lincoln Memorial. Clinton chose the route that Thomas Jefferson took when he traveled from Charlottesville to Washington, because he said of the third president: "He was sort of associated with the populism of his time." As the procession rode along Interstate 66, the Virginia Department of Transportation put up sequential Burma Shave–like signs:

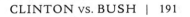
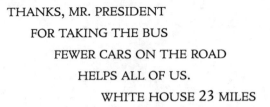

THANKS, MR. PRESIDENT
FOR TAKING THE BUS
FEWER CARS ON THE ROAD
HELPS ALL OF US.
WHITE HOUSE 23 MILES

THE ELECTION OF 1996

WILLIAM J. CLINTON, Democrat
47.2 million (379 electoral) Albert A. Gore Jr.

BOB DOLE, Republican
39.2 million (159 electoral) Jack F. Kemp

H. ROSS PEROT, Reform Party
8.1 million (0 electoral) Patrick J. Choate

The election of 1996 found the nation in a state of relative calm, with no formidable foreign threats and an economy that remained strong. The Democrats easily nominated Clinton and Gore for second terms while the Republicans sifted through a bevy of possible candidates, including Pat Buchanan; *Forbes* magazine's editor in chief, Steve Forbes; talk-radio host Alan Keyes; Senator Arlen Specter, California governor Pete Wilson; and one-time Supreme Court nominee Robert Bork, eventually putting Bob Dole forward as their choice.

Much of the campaign's best humor centered on Gore's self-deprecating style. In a speech to several thousand California delegates, Gore related some amusing comments made about his legendary stiff demeanor:

" 'He's so stiff, racks buy their suits off Al Gore.'

" 'If you use a strobe light, it looks like Al Gore is actually moving.'

" 'Al Gore is an inspiration to millions of Americans who suffer from Dutch elm disease.'

"I've heard them all," Gore told the laughing crowd, "and each time I say, 'Very funny, Tipper.' "

The election also drew several fringe candidates, including

the U.S. Green Party's Ralph Nader and, once again Ross Perot, who ran on the Reform Party ticket.

Without any opposition, Clinton was able to start his campaign in the summer and immediately portrayed Dole, who was nominated in August, as feeble and unexciting. Indeed, compared with the healthy fifty-year-old Clinton, Dole was undynamic and had several mishaps, including falling off a stage and referring to baseball games that had occurred decades earlier as if they were recently played. Unlike Reagan, Dole was unable to overcome many voters' belief that he was not up to the physical and mental rigors of being president.

In contrast with the 1992 election, Perot was locked out of the televised debates, which saw Clinton against Dole and Al Gore against former professional football player and congressman Jack Kemp.

The campaign was marred by allegations lodged against the Democrats of illegal fund-raising, especially an incident in which Gore received money raised at a Buddhist temple in California—a violation of religious groups' tax-exempt status. One Democratic National Committee fund-raiser was convicted of the charge, and the Democratic National Committee had to return $100,000 in donations.

As the campaign played out, Democrats continued to portray Dole as out of touch and mean-spirited. He hurt his campaign because he was not particularly good at speaking without a script, despite the fact that those who know him say he has an excellent sense of humor. On the other side, Clinton was energetic and could talk for an hour extemporaneously.

Polls gave Dole high marks for integrity and honesty, in contrast with Clinton's low marks in these areas.

Clinton scored a decisive victory over Dole, with Perot receiving less than half as many votes as he had in 1992. Perot did not receive any electoral votes, the same result as the previous election.

· · · · · · · · · ·

During their first debate Dole criticized President Clinton for his ad-hoc approach to handling foreign affairs. He described it this way:

"Well, we get up in the morning and read the papers and [see] what country is in trouble."

Clinton's integrity was a feature of this election, and Dole capitalized on it with this one:

"If something happened along the route and you had to leave your children with Bob Dole or Bill Clinton, I think you would probably leave them with Bob Dole."

During a C-SPAN broadcast Dole said:

"You know, 'A Better Man for a Better America.' That's sort of our slogan."

During the second debate, Dole made a huge mistake when he characterized the country's economy under Clinton as "the worst economy in a century." This raised many eyebrows and a few laughs, as he seemed to be discounting the Great Depression of the 1930s.

When Texas senator Phil Gramm was asked if he would have a woman as his running mate, he said:

"Sophia Loren is not a citizen."

At a fund-raising event in Texas, Gramm said to his supporters:

"We are one victory away from getting our money back."

LOCAL COLOR

"The dirty work at political conventions is almost always done in the grim hours between midnight and dawn. Hangmen and politicians work best when the human spirit is at its lowest ebb."
—*Satirist Russell Baker*

"I am sure that many political candidates are defeated because the public has been given an opportunity to see what they look like. The next great political victory will be achieved by the party that is smart enough to have nobody heading the ticket."
—*Groucho Marx*

Somewhat cynical about the election process, Gramm said:
"I have the most reliable friend you can have in American politics, and that is ready money."

Dole's press secretary, Nelson Warfield, was trying to quell criticism that his candidate was too old and out of touch. He said:

"People are more interested in a strong economy than someone who can tell you if Hootie & the Blowfish are going to have a strong album next time."

Said Pat Buchanan of Dole:

"Bob Dole is our Walter Mondale. He's the weakest front-runner I've seen in a long time."

Funnyman Harry Shearer on why Dole's age was not a factor in the election:

"He's married to the head of the American Red Cross, so he can get fresh blood whenever he wants."

Said newspaper columnist Mike Royko about Dole's public image:

"It's Dole's misfortune that when he does smile, he looks as if he's just evicted a widow."

Buchanan described Tennessee governor and secretary of education Lamar Alexander as "the fellow who goes around in the Howdy Doody shirt."

Lamar Alexander said of Steve Forbes, son of the famous Malcolm Forbes and publisher of the magazine that bears his name, during a debate in Columbia, South Carolina:

"You should go practice your dirty business on a race for the school board before you try for the presidency of the United States."

About two years before the election, Barry Goldwater made this comment about Dole's possible candidacy:

"He's got a mean little temper. Maybe he ought to go home."

During a campaign trip through Montana and Colorado, Clinton noted:

"Look, half the time when I see the evening news, I wouldn't be for me either."

In discussing his chances for the Republican nomination, Lamar Alexander invoked the name of Kato Kaelin, a neighbor of O. J. Simpson whose testimony in the case brought him instant notoriety:

"I am encouraged by the example of Kato Kaelin, who was relatively unknown until two weeks ago."

Bob Dole said of Lamar Alexander, who claimed to be an "outsider":

"Lamar's out there every day claiming he's the outsider. I remember meeting him when I came to Washington."

On withdrawing from the race, Phil Gramm said:

"When the voters speak, I listen. Especially when the voter is saying someone else's name."

During a debate, the following exchange occurred between Bob Dole and Steve Forbes:

DOLE: Steve, you've got to defend me. Someone has to defend me.

FORBES: Well, Senator, you've been on the payroll for thirty-five years; if you can't defend yourself now, I can't help you.

Discussing his plan to put government on a better economic footing, Dole stated far too casually:

"Reining in government and all that other stuff."

Phil Gramm was being honest when he said of his qualifications for becoming president:

"There are probably a couple hundred thousand people who could do a better job."

Joked Dole: "We've never had a president named Bob. And I think it's time."

During a photo-op-only event, Dole said:

"We're trying to get good pictures. Don't worry very much about what I say."

If elected, Buchanan said his first act as president would be to arrest Bill Clinton. Buchanan mocked Clinton's long-windedness:

"Sir, you have the right to remain silent."

Noting that the other candidates, including Newt Gingrich, Phil Gramm, and Bob Dole, had all been divorced and re-married, Jay Leno said:

"Wouldn't it be funny if, of all the candidates, Bill Clinton had the best marriage?"

When asked why he and Bob Dole agreed to discuss national issues on *60 Minutes,* Clinton said:

"We're too old for *Survivor* and *Star Search.*"

In describing Jack Kemp's decision to be Bob Dole's running mate, the director of California's Democratic Party, Bob Mulholland, said: "I think Jack Kemp just got into the passenger seat of the last scene of *Thelma & Louise.*"

Saying that he wasn't too old to run for president, because Senator Strom Thurmond was in his seventies and still going strong, Dole said:

"Every time I look at Strom Thurmond, I'm inspired. . . . When I see him eat a banana, I eat a banana."

Speaking of his health, Dole said: "My cholesterol's lower than Clinton's, my blood pressure's lower than Clinton's, my weight is less than Clinton's. I am not going to make health an issue."

Clinton responded to this by saying: "My pulse rate is much lower than Dole's, but I don't have to deal with Phil Gramm every day."

Gore led with his intelligence when he told Kemp before a debate in St. Petersburg, Florida:

"I'd like to start by offering you a deal, Jack. If you won't use any . . . football stories, I won't tell any of my warm and humorous stories about . . . chlorofluorocarbon abatement."

Dole left the Senate to run for president, noting:

"I will seek the presidency with nothing to fall back on but the judgment of the people and with nowhere to go but the White House or home."

Campaigning for Dole at a robotics factory, George H. W. Bush said:

"The defense budget is more than a piggy bank for people who want to get busy beating swords into pork barrels."

Conceding defeat, Dole said:

"It's a lot more fun winning. It hurts to lose."

THE ELECTION OF 2000

GEORGE W. BUSH, Republican
50,456 million (271 electoral) Richard B. Cheney

AL GORE, Democrat
50,999 million (266 electoral) Joseph I. Lieberman

RALPH NADER, Green Party
2. 9 million (0 electoral) Winona LaDuke

Wow. What can you say about an election that was the most controversial and closest presidential contest in U.S. history—an outcome that still angers many Americans?

Thank goodness for politicians who kept us entertained with their malapropisms and jokes.

With the voting booths closed and the race too close to call, the final tally rested on Florida's electoral votes, but it was not a simple matter of just counting the ballots. Voter fraud was alleged as television viewers watched recount after recount of paper ballots with so-called hanging chads—the name given to punched-out paper ballot pieces that were in question. Was the paper circle or oval piece fully punched out, indicating a vote, or was it punched out and barely hanging, indicating a no-vote?

Late-night comics had a field day making fun of these bits of paper and Bush's quirky misspeaks. Just days before the election, Bush gave a speech in St. Charles, Missouri, during which he stated, "They want the federal government controlling Social Security like it's some kind of federal program." And during the second presidential debate with Gore, Bush said this of education initiatives: "I mean, there needs to be a wholesale effort against racial profiling, which is illiterate children."

With a race so close, voters around the country were fuming that the nation's fate rested on antiquated voting systems that were prone to human error and subject to their discretion or opinion, especially in an already contentious atmosphere.

On November 8, the Florida Division of Elections reported that Texas governor George W. Bush and his running mate, Richard Cheney, former secretary of defense under the first President Bush, had a margin of victory of 1,784 votes. Because it was less than 0.5 percent of the votes cast, Florida law called for an automatic machine recount. The recount showed Bush's lead was only 327 votes.

Because Florida law allows a candidate to request a manual count, Gore and his running mate, Connecticut senator Joseph Lieberman, asked for recounts in four counties: Palm Beach, Broward, Miami-Dade, and Volusia. The manual recount began, and the hanging chad was born. But Florida law also required that counties certify their returns within seven days of the election, and courts ruled that they could amend their returns if necessary. With the deadline past, Florida secretary of state Katherine Harris certified returns from all sixty-seven counties, even though Palm Beach, Broward, and Miami-Dade were still recounting. Harris then set criteria to judge whether a late count was justified and denied extensions for these counties.

The case went to the Supreme Court, which ruled that the recount procedure was unconstitutional because it applied different counting standards to different counties.

In the final tally, Bush won Florida by only 537 votes.

Charges of Bush stealing the election only got more vocal when it was learned that although Bush won the electoral vote 271 to 266 (a D.C. electoral voter had left her ballot blank to protest the District's lack of congressional representation), he lost the popular vote by about a half million votes.

Ralph Nader, candidate of the Green Party, garnered almost 3 million votes but no electoral votes, and some Gore supporters claimed that his entry into the race allowed Bush to win. Nader was dubbed a "spoiler." Other colorful characters took a stab in the primaries (or at least thought about it), including Donald Trump and Pat Buchanan. For example, a reporter asked Trump how he was different from other candidates, and he replied: "I think the only difference between me and the other candidates is that I'm more honest and my women are more beautiful."

Despite the rancor surrounding this election, stand-up comedians had a great time making fun of the participants involved. Also, because of the growth of the Internet, jokes and one-liners about the election were flying around the world to an extent not seen in any other election. Indeed, much of the humor about this rather nonhumorous election came from those other than the candidates.

· · · · · · · · ·

Gore and Bush exchanged e-mails shortly after they received their respective party's nomination. Bush sent a sarcastic e-mail to Gore, rejecting his proposal to ban campaign ads funded by unregulated "soft money." The message also mocked Gore for his once claiming that he invented the Internet:

"Thank you for your email. This Internet of yours is a wonderful invention," Bush wrote. [Gore actually said, "During my service in the United States Congress, I took the initiative in creating the Internet," which was true.]

Making light of his comments about inventing the Internet, Gore told David Letterman:

"Remember, America: I gave you the Internet, and I can take it away."

While watching an altercation during the South Carolina primary, Senator John McCain said:

"That's what happens when you get your staff from prison work-release programs."

LOCAL COLOR

"You shouldn't be governor unless you can pronounce the name of the state."
—*California governor Gray Davis during the 2003 recall campaign, making fun of Arnold Schwarzenegger's "Kah-lee-fohr-nyah" pronunciation*

"I think I Could Bring Some New Blood to the Office."
—*Campaign slogan of Mike Pulliam in 1988 who lost his race for coroner of Hughes County, South Dakota*

During a debate, Bush said to Gore:

"Mr. Vice President, in all due respect, it is—I'm not sure eighty percent of the people will get the death tax. I know this: A hundred percent will get it if I'm the president."

Speaking in Nashua just a few days before the New Hampshire primary, Bush was trying to show the economic plight of single working mothers when he said they were "working hard to put food on your family."

On several occasions, Bush used the world "tollbooth" when he meant "roadblock," as in this instance during the New Hampshire primary when he said that taxes were too high:

"It's not fair! It's a tollbooth on the road to the middle class, and I intend not only to reduce the fees but to knock the tollbooth down."

Said Utah's Orrin Hatch during the presidential campaign:

"It's time for Bill, Hillary, and Al to go home—if they can just figure out where home is."

Appearing on *Oprah* before the election, Bush said:

"I am a person who recognizes the fallacy of humans."

Republican contender Alan Keyes was trying to make a point when he said:

"If I were to lose my mind right now and pick up one of you and dash your head against the floor and kill you, would that be right?"

During the Republican primary, Bush said of McCain:

"The senator has got to understand if he's going to have— He can't have it both ways. He can't take the high horse and then claim the low road."

Steve Forbes said of the Internal Revenue Service:

"Only in Washington would anyone call the IRS a 'service.'"

LOCAL COLOR

"Only a governor can make executions happen. I did. And I will."
—*Texas governor Mark White, campaigning for reelection in 1990*

"If you allow me to license and regulate marijuana, I'll fill every hotel and motel room in the state of Kentucky."
—*Gatewood Galbraith, running for governor in 1991 on his plan to increase tourism*

After McCain dropped out of the race, he and Bush had a meeting during which he said:

"I think we agree, the past is over."

During the Republican primary, Bush said:

"We need to make the pie higher."

During the campaign, Bush said to host Chris Matthews on
Hardball:

"I'm gonna talk about the ideal world, Chris. I've
read— I understand reality. If you're asking me as the president, would I understand reality, I do."

Asked if he would like to take back any comments he made
during the presidential debates, Bush said:

"I think if you know what you believe, it makes it a lot
easier to answer questions. I can't answer your question."

Speaking in Hilton Head, South Carolina, Bush said:

"If you're sick and tired of the politics of cynicism and
polls and principles, come and join this campaign."

Republican contender Elizabeth Dole said:

"Only one thing would be worse than the status quo.
And that would be for the status quo to become the norm."

Bush apparently meant "subliminal messages." Instead:

"The idea of putting subliminable messages into ads is
ridiculous."

Bob Dole was discussing allegations of impropriety in
Gore's fund-raising and said:

"You can see through that like you can [Jennifer]
Lopez's dress."

Bush was discussing Internet millionaires, those "who have
become rich beyond their means."

Jesse Jackson admonished voters: "There's more with Gore! Stay out of the Bushes!"

Joseph Lieberman made light of Bush's lack of economic acumen with this one:

"His economic plan could fit on the back of a shampoo bottle: Cut taxes, increase spending, borrow, repeat."

Being Jewish, Lieberman does not attend church on Sunday, a detail lost on Louisiana senator John Breaux:

"I think people don't care so much where he goes to church on Sunday, but just that he has the moral values and principles to lead this country."

Gore pulled a fast one on the crowd with:

"I did think it was effective when I weaved in stories of real people from the audience and their everyday challenges. Like the woman here tonight whose husband is about to lose his job. She is struggling to get out of public housing and get a job on her own. Hillary Clinton, I want to fight for you!"

Gore's wife, Tipper, asked voters to support her husband's bid for candidate with this:

"It's not *The Dating Game*. . . . You don't have to fall in love with Al Gore; I did that."

Actor and movie director Rob Reiner said of the Bush–Cheney candidacy:

"This is how they define diversity? Having two guys to lead the ticket from two different oil companies?"

When the election results were still in doubt and hinging on Florida's final count, Gore said to Bush about Florida governor Jeb Bush's affirmation that his state went for George:

"Let me explain something to you. Your brother is not the ultimate authority on this."

In 1999, Bush was pilloried in the media for not knowing the names of the leaders of Chechnya, Taiwan, India, or Pakistan. Gore later joked to a radio audience:

"But not knowing the names . . . I think that's kind of understandable. I mean, the other day I was talking to Otkir Sultonov. You know, the prime minister of Uzbekistan. And he asked me, 'Did you send a birthday card to Hamed?' That's of course Hamed Karoui, the prime minister of Tunisia. I had just been talking about him with Ion Sturza, the prime minister of Moldova. We're old friends. We actually met through a mutual friend, Lennart Meri—the president of Estonia, of course."

When asked about his loss for the presidency, Gore mentioned kissing his wife, Tipper, onstage after receiving the nomination:

"I often get asked the question: 'Is there anything I would have done differently?' I say, 'Yeah, there is. If I had to do it over again, I would have kissed Tipper longer.' "

Donna Brazile, Gore's campaign manager, said:

"Republicans bring out Colin Powell and J. C. Watts because they have no program, no policy. They have no love and no joy. They'd rather take pictures with black children than feed them."

At the Democratic convention Gore characterized the Republican Party this way:

"We're the party of Tomorrowland. They're the party of Fantasyland. We're the party of Main Street U.S.A. They're the party of the Pirates of Enron."

LOCAL COLOR

"Our United States Senate is just chock full of song-and-dance men—sixty-two of them. They are called lawyers and David 'Porky' Boren is one of them. Isn't there room in this exclusive club of male clowns for a real honest-to-goodness clown?"
—*Oklahoma senate candidate Virginia Jenner, on why she wore a clown suit during the 1990 campaign*

"A coup attempt by the Taliban element of the California Republican Party."
—*California Democratic Party director Bob Mulholland, on the 2003 California election recall*

In early May 2000, Bush showed reporters in his campaign plane a story in the *Weekly World News* that featured a photograph of Bush shaking hands with a space alien. The headline read SPACE ALIEN BACKS BUSH FOR PRESIDENT! Bush noted that his alien encounter was further proof that the Republican Party had wide appeal: "New faces, new voices. It goes to show I'm willing to reach across certain demographic lines."

In July 2000, Bush talked with the media on board his campaign plane:

"I don't read half of what you write," he admitted.

"We don't listen to half of what you say," one of the reporters said.

"That's apparent in the other half of what I read," Bush replied.

When asked what he would say in his acceptance speech at the convention, Bush said, "I thought I would start off with 'I accept your nomination.' It might not be very original, but it seems to get a good applause."

Assessing the polls, Bush said: "The good news is, we're ahead in the polls. The bad news is that the election isn't tomorrow."

Months before his choice of Senator Joe Lieberman as his running mate, Gore spoke before the Anti-Defamation League and attempted an old-fashioned Catskill Mountains–type routine. He said that a new subgenre of music was emerging in Nashville: The Jewish country-western song:

"Reaching number four on the charts was 'I Was One of the Chosen People—Until She Chose Somebody Else.' Number three: 'The Second Time She Said "Shalom," I

Knew She Meant Good-bye.' Number two: 'I've Got My Foot on the Glass, Now Where Are You?'" And number one, which Gore actually sang, was "'Mommas, Don't Let Your Ungrateful Sons Grow Up to Be Cowboys When They Could Very Easily Just Have Taken Over the Family Business That My Own Grandfather Broke His Back to Start and My Father Sweated Over the Years, Which Apparently Doesn't Mean Anything Now That You're Turning Your Back on Such a Gift.'"

David Letterman's "Top Ten Rejected Gore–Lieberman Campaign Slogans," as read by Gore on the show:

10. Vote for me, or I'll come to your home and explain my 191-page economic plan to you in excruciating detail.

9. Remember, America, I gave you the Internet, and I can take it away!

8. Your vote automatically enters you in a drawing for the $123-billion-dollar surplus.

7. With Lieberman on the ticket, you get all kinds of fun new days off.

6. We know when the microphone is on.

5. Vote for me, and I will take whatever steps necessary to outlaw the term, "Whazzzup?"

4. Gore–Lieberman—you don't have to worry about pork barrel politics.

3. You'll thank us in four years when the escalator to the moon is finished.

2. If I can handle Letterman, I can handle Saddam Hussein.

1. I'll be twice as cool as that president guy on *The West Wing*.

Several years before the election Donald Trump was asked if he would make a good president. He said on *Evans & Novak*:

"I'm too forthright. I'm too— I think I'm too honest. But I do believe I'm too forthright to be a politician."

About Buchanan losing the Republican nomination, Trump said:

"We have no choice but to assume that had Buchanan been president, he would have allowed Hitler to wage uncontested war on defenseless civilian populations. We must also assume that Buchanan would have conducted his policy with the belief that Hitler had no ill-will toward the United States. He would have been our version of Neville Chamberlain."

Trump countered criticism that his bid for president was just for fun by saying:

"For those who suggest that this [presidential bid] has just been a promotion, I want to strongly deny that."

Commenting on the other third-party candidates, Trump said:

"The Reform Party now includes a Klansman, Mr. Duke;

a neo-Nazi, Mr. Buchanan; and a Communist, Ms. Fulani. This is not company I wish to keep."

"Since the beginning of my political exploratory effort, I have consistently said that I was only interested in running if I had the prospect of winning. Without Jesse [Jackson], the Reform Party is just an extremist shell and cannot be a force or even a factor in 2000."

While he was mulling over whether to run for president, Trump noted:

"I'm not prepared to throw [my money] away. I'd rather go to Atlantic City and take a bet on the tables, because, to be honest with you, unless there's total unity in this party, it would be foolhardy to run."

Discussing the two major-party candidates, Trump said:

"I'd really like to make the race, particularly if the nominees are 'Gush' and 'Bore.'"

Trump noted this difference between his campaign and others, because Trump was able to glean public relations return from his investment:

"Ours is the only presidential campaign that makes money."

Trump makes an interesting point here:

"For years, I watched politicians brag how poor they were, how poor their family is, how poor their grandparents were, and how their families have been losers for years and years. 'And, elect me, because I'm a loser.' "

Trump's plan for balancing the budget was by levying a 14.25-percent tax on the net worth of the wealthy, which would raise about $6 trillion and wipe out the national debt immediately:

"The plan I am proposing today does not involve smoke and mirrors, phony numbers, financial gimmicks, or the usual economic chicanery you usually find in Disneyland-on-the-Potomac."

LOCAL COLOR

Bob Dole tells this story: "Two newly elected Democratic congressmen were discussing campaign tactics. One insisted that it was very important to gain the support of taxi drivers, because they spoke with hundreds of passengers each day. The congressman told how he would engage in friendly conversations with cabdrivers, compliment their driving skills, and leave them a large tip. As they drove away, the congressman would shout: 'Vote Democrat.'

"The other Democratic congressman said he did something a little bit different. 'Before I leave the cab, I toss a lighted match on the backseat, slash the tires, and spit on the window. Then I stick my head in on the driver's side and shout, 'Vote Republican.' "

After a strong beginning, Buchanan's primary campaign had declined, and comedian Dennis Miller noted:

"He got his butt kicked on Super Tuesday. I hope it doesn't cause brain damage." Added the acerbic Miller: "Pat Buchanan doesn't want to create a third party. A Third Reich, maybe."

On those who voted for Buchanan proportedly to snub their noses at the two main parties, Dennis Miller observed:

"A lot of people voting for Pat Buchanan say they are doing so to send a message. Apparently that message is, 'Hey, look at me, I'm an idiot.'"

Bush said in Bentonville, Arkansas, just a day before the election:

"They misunderestimated me."

During an interview with Jim Lehrer of the *NewsHour with Jim Lehrer* the following exchange took place:

Bush: I talked to my little brother, Jeb— I haven't told this to many people, but he's the governor of— I wouldn't call him my little brother—my brother, Jeb, the great governor of Texas.

Lehrer: Florida.

Bush: Florida. The state of the Florida.

During a debate in St. Louis, Bush said:

"Drug therapies are replacing a lot of medicines as we used to know it."

During a campaign stop in Saginaw, Michigan, Bush said:

"I know the human being and fish can coexist peacefully."

Discussing vice-presidential candidate Cheney, *Nightline*'s Ted Koppel asked:

"So he's your lightning rod?"

Bush responded: "More than that, he's my sounding rod."

Deriding his opponent's strategy, Bush said of Gore:

"The fact that he relies on facts—says things that are not factual—are going to undermine his campaign."

As quoted in the *Austin-American Statesman*, Bush said this a few days before the election:

"If you don't stand for anything, you don't stand for anything. If you don't stand for something, you don't stand for anything."

During a presidential campaign stop in Los Angeles, California, Bush said:

"I was raised in the west. The west of Texas. It's pretty close to California. In more ways than Washington, D.C., is close to California."

About a month before the election, Bush discussed how he would handle the issue of dependency on foreign sources for oil:

"I've been talking to Vicente Fox, the new president of

Mexico—I know him—to have gas and oil sent to the United States . . . so we'll not depend on foreign oil."

From a speech delivered by Bush in Arlington Heights, Illinois:

"It's important for us to explain to our nation that life is important. It's not only of babies, but it's of children living in, you know, the dark dungeons of the Internet."

When speculation arose as early as 1998 about whether George W. Bush, then still governor of Texas, would seek the Republican nomination, he said:

"There is a lot of speculation, and I guess there is going to continue to be a lot of speculation until the speculation ends."

At a campaign speech in Kalamazoo, Michigan, Bush said:

"Now, by the way, surplus means a little money left over. Otherwise it wouldn't be called a surplus."

When asked about the outcome of the 2000 election that ended with the Supreme Court decision, Carol Moseley Braun, the first black female senator, said:

"It was the black vote that decided the 2000 election—Clarence Thomas."

Bush meant this comment as a joke when he appeared about a month before the election at the Al Smith Memorial Dinner in New York:

"And I see Bill Buckley is here tonight—a fellow Yale

man. We go way back, and we have a lot in common. Bill wrote a book at Yale, and I read one."

During the first presidential debate, Bush said of Gore:
"Look, this is a man. He's got great numbers. He talks about numbers. I'm beginning to think not only did he invent the Internet, but he invented the calculator."

And another one on the same subject:
"You've heard Al Gore say he invented the Internet. Well, if he was so smart, why do all the addresses begin with 'W'?"

During a campaign speech in Des Moines, Iowa, Bush said:
"This campaign not only hears the voices of the entrepreneurs and the farmers but we hear the voices of those struggling to get ahead."

CBS's Dan Rather came up with these great lines to describe election night:
"This race is shakier than cafeteria Jell-O."
"Turn the lights down, the party just got wilder."
"It's cardiac-arrest time in this presidential campaign."
"He swept through the South like a tornado through a trailer park."
"Don't bet the trailer money yet."
"Now, Florida, that race, the heat from it is hot enough to peel house paint."
"This will have the people in Austin standing up like they got stuck with hat pins."

"Frankly, we don't know whether to wind the watch or to bark at the moon."

"We've lived by the crystal ball, we're eating so much broken glass. We're in critical condition."

After losing the election, Gore was fond of joking:

"I am Al Gore, and I used to be the next president of the United States of America."

THE ELECTION OF 2004

GEORGE W. BUSH, Republican
62.0 million (286 electoral) Richard B. Cheney

JOHN F. KERRY, Democrat
59.0 million (251 electoral) John Edwards

The main issue of the 2004 election was the U.S.-led invasion of Iraq and President Bush's response to the attacks on the World Trade Center and the Pentagon on September 11, 2001. The president's approval ratings soared after 9/11 as Americans approved of the U.S. attack on alleged al-Qaeda bases in Afghanistan.

Americans also supported Bush's decision to invade Iraq in March 2003, which was marked by a lightning-fast ground invasion from the south, the taking of Baghdad, and overthrowing dictator Saddam Hussein.

Bush's opponent was Vietnam veteran John Kerry, senator from Massachusetts, who hammered away at Bush's lack of military service and low interest in domestic issues such as health-care reform and tax relief for the middle and lower classes. Kerry said of George Bush's running for a second term, "All over the country people are asking whether or not George Bush is smart enough to be president of the United States. And the scary thing is, one of the people asking me was Dan Quayle."

Bush attacked Kerry as a "flip-flopper" who praised the Iraq invasion on the one hand yet seemed to say that it was unneeded. In the Senate, Kerry had voted in favor of funding the invasion and now was changing his mind. Kerry was portrayed as conflicted over Iraq, as opposed to Bush, who was resolute in his thinking, and a majority of the American public responded to the president's message.

The debates were lively, with both sides claiming victory. Kerry zinged Bush with this one during a debate: "I'm glad the president finally found an economic development program. I'm just sad that it's only in Baghdad." One of the odd moments of the debates was afterward, when photos began circulating on the Web that showed a mysterious lump in the back of Bush's suit jacket. Supporters claimed it was simply a pucker in the material while detractors said it was a radio receiver that allowed Bush to be coached—a reference to him being a "lightweight."

As with the 2000 election, 2004 saw the final count hinge on one state. This time Ohio was in the spotlight, with its electoral votes not fully certified until the day after the election, thus giving Bush the victory. Democrats alleged voter fraud and manipulation, but in the final vote Bush and Cheney won the election. One ardent Minnesota elector cast a single electoral vote for John Edwards for president.

As with the previous election, the Internet provided the bulk of the humor as hundreds of Web sites were built to accommodate jokes, humorous videos, and hilarious Photoshopped pictures of the candidates.

· · · · · · · · · ·

Presidential candidate Al Gore decided not to run in 2004 but he did give a speech at the Democratic National Convention:

"I had hoped to be back here this week under different

circumstances, running for reelection. But you know the old saying: You win some, you lose some. And then there's that little-known third category. I didn't come here tonight to talk about the past. After all, I don't want you to think I lie awake at night counting and recounting sheep. I prefer to focus on the future because I know from my own experience that America is a land of opportunity, where every little boy and girl has a chance to grow up and win the popular vote."

Speaking about Bush losing the popular vote in the 2000 election, Lieberman said:

"I know I can beat George Bush [in 2004]. Why? Because Al Gore and I already did."

Late-night comedian Conan O'Brien said:

"The presidential campaign is getting kind of ugly—did you hear about this? Yesterday, a twenty-seven-year-old woman came forward to deny rumors that she had an affair with Democratic front-runner John Kerry. The woman added, 'I would never cheat on Bill Clinton.'"

Comedian Dennis Miller on handicapping the 2004 election:

"I haven't seen a starting nine like that since the '62 Mets."

Talk-show host Laura Ingraham said of candidate Kerry:

"One is reminded that [John Kerry] is really just a better-looking Ted Kennedy, a richer Michael Dukakis."

Making light of the fact that Kerry's wife, Teresa, heir to the Heinz family fortune, asked him to sign a prenuptial agreement, talk-show host Sean Hannity said:

"If his wife doesn't trust him, why should you?"

During the Congressional Black Caucus presidential debate, Al Sharpton said:

"I'm a man of action. And unlike Schwarzenegger, I never had a stunt man do my hard work."

At a presidential debate forum, Sharpton noted:

"We've been told we had three minutes. My good friend Senator Edwards spoke for five. So Joe Lieberman told me that, in the spirit of affirmative action, I get seven."

Democratic hopeful Howard Dean was asked if it would be a problem for him to understand black voters because there are so few African Americans in Vermont. He responded:

"If the percentage of minorities that's in your state has anything to do with how you connect with African American voters, then Trent Lott would be Martin Luther King."

Al Sharpton was addressing the Tawana Brawley scandal when he said:

"The next time anybody wants to know about Tawana Brawley, I'm going to ask them, 'Do you ask Teddy Kennedy about Chappaquiddick? Do you ask Hillary Clinton about her husband?'"

Hoping that Bush would lose his bid for a second term, Richard Gephardt rhymed:

"Like father, like son; four years and he's done."

Speaking to the California Democratic Party, John Edwards knew what he wanted to say, but it came out:

"Like many of us, I grew up in a small town in North Carolina."

Defending his decision to change his position from pro-life to pro-choice, Dennis Kucinich said:

"The position I'm taking now is an expansion, not reversal."

Richard Gephardt had this to say to Howard Dean about his sometimes eccentric behavior:

"You've been saying for many months that you're the head of the Democratic wing of the Democratic Party. I think you're just winging it."

Kerry's campaign manager Jim Jordan dissed primary candidate Howard Dean by saying:

"Ultimately, voters are going to decide a small-town physician from a small and atypical state is probably not qualified to lead this nation in a dangerous world."

Howard Dean defended himself against those who said he was too much of an oddball to run for president:

"To listen to Senator Lieberman, Senator Kerry, Representative Gephardt, I'm anti-Israel, I'm anti-trade, I'm anti-Medicare, and I'm anti–Social Security. I wonder how I ended up in the Democratic Party."

Edwards repelled notions that he was too well turned out to run for vice president. He told one group about a newspaper columnist who likened him to a Ken doll:

"A Ken doll is plastic, lacking in substance, and can be bought for about ten dollars. There's at least one critical difference right there."

When asked if he supported gay marriage Sharpton replied:

"That's like asking me, do I support black marriage or white marriage?"

When asked what he thought of Al Gore's chances for running in and winning an election in 2004, Senator Christopher Dodd of Connecticut said:

"I'm changing the subject real quickly here."

Speaking about Bush's jobs policy, John Edwards noted:

"The president goes around the country speaking Spanish. The only Spanish he speaks when it comes to jobs is 'Hasta la vista.'"

Sharpton said:

"Bush said after September 11, we've got to go after [Osama] bin Laden. Yet he can't find bin Laden. . . . He can't find the weapons. Now we've got to take pride that Saddam Hussein is still alive; we can't find him. I promise you, if I'm elected, President Bush will not be in charge of the missing persons bureau."

In a moment of self-deprecating humor, Edwards said on *The Daily Show*, of his bid for the presidential nomination:

"I don't know if you've been following the polls. But I think it will actually be news to most people that I'm running for president of the United States."

Gephardt was asked his qualifications for debating George Bush. He responded:

"I can put two sentences together, and I know I can pronounce the word 'nuclear.'"

LOCAL COLOR

"During a political campaign, everyone is concerned with what a candidate will do on this or that question if he is elected, except the candidate; he's too busy wondering what he'll do if he isn't elected."
—*Everett Dirksen, senator from Illinois, 1950–1969*

During a speech in New Hampshire, Kerry quipped:

"What we need now is not just a regime change in Saddam Hussein and Iraq, but we need a regime change in the United States."

Kerry said this about Bush:

"I promise just to serve two terms. Republicans do it differently. They just have the son repeat the father's whole first term."

Democratic strategist and former Clinton staffer Paul Begala summed up Bush's candidacy this way:

"If you don't think it's a gamble to put a man in the White House who believes we should have guns in church, who thinks the Taliban is a rock band, who was such a failure as a businessman that his company was nicknamed 'El-Busto,' who wants to turn our Social Security system into a Wall Street boiler room, who can't name a single thing he disagrees with Jerry Falwell and Pat Robertson on, who smeared a bona fide hero named John McCain, and whose principal policy proposal is to give America's surplus to the idle rich in the form of a $1.3-trillion tax cut, you're either nuts or a Republican."

On the possibility of running with Pat Buchanan, Joseph Lieberman said:

"Lieberman–Buchanan: a ticket only a mother could love. Lieberman–Buchanan: building a bridge to the fourteenth century."

Howard Dean said of his relations with the African American community:

"I have in some ways a special relationship with the African American community because of my college career. I had two African American roommates in college."

On Bush's plan to cut taxes, Sharpton said:

"It was like Jim Jones giving out Kool-Aid. It tastes good, but it will kill you."

About Bush's "trickle-down" theory of economics, Kerry said:

"I believe every worker in America is tired of being trickled on by George W. Bush."

Donald Trump made this observation on CNN a few months before the election:

"And it just seems that the economy does better under the Democrats than the Republicans. Now, it shouldn't be that way. But if you go back, I mean it just seems that the economy does better under the Democrats."

Filmmaker Michael Moore, as quoted in *Entertainment Weekly*, said:

"I mean, this is a party [Democrats] that can't even win when they win. They lose when they win; you can't get more pathetic than that. We have to save them from themselves."

On election night, CBS's Dan Rather came up with these gems:

"This race is hotter than a Times Square Rolex."
"His lead is as thin as turnip soup."
"The presidential race is swinging like Count Basie."
"This race is hotter than the devil's anvil."

"One's reminded of that old saying, 'Don't taunt the alligator until after you've crossed the creek.'"

"This situation in Ohio would give an aspirin a headache."

"No one is saying that George Bush is not going to win the election, and if you had to bet the double-wide, you'd have to bet that he'd win."

"In Southern states they beat him like a rented mule."

There was much negotiation about the presidential debate. Kerry said this on *David Letterman:*

"I wanted to have John Edwards stand. Dick Cheney wanted to sit. We compromised, and now George Bush is gonna sit on Dick Cheney's lap."

John Kerry talking to Regis Philbin about the debate:

"The big hang-up was George Bush wanted to get lifelines—you know, so he could call somebody."

Kerry on the almost-final tally:

"Here I am in the state of New Mexico. George Bush is still in the state of denial. New Mexico has five electoral votes. The state of denial has none. I like my chances."

From John Kerry's speech entitled "Science and Innovation" in Columbus, Ohio:

"You get the feeling that if George Bush had been president during other periods in American history, he would have sided with the candle lobby against electricity, the buggy-makers against cars, and typewriter companies against computers."

Kerry said of Bush's Iraq strategy:

"Invading Iraq in response to 9/11 would be like Franklin Roosevelt invading Mexico in response to Pearl Harbor."

On the surrealism of electioneering, Kerry said:

"You'd be amazed at the number of people who want to introduce themselves to you in the men's room. It's the most bizarre part of this entire thing."

On board Kerry's refurbished Boeing 757, used for campaigning:

"In the event of emergency, my hair can be used as a flotation device."

On Bush's political adviser Karl Rove, Kerry said:

"I figured out Karl Rove's political strategy—make gas so expensive that no Democrats can afford to go to the polls."

Acknowledgments

I am most grateful for the creative assistance of Larry Kahaner, Bill Adler, Will Schwalbe, and Brendan Duffy for making this book possible, and a special thanks to Bob Miller at Hyperion for leading the way.

Charles Osgood

NEW YORK